Play Therapy: A Do-It-Yourself Guide for Practitioners

by Jay Cerio, Ph.D.

© 2000
Lea R. Powell Institute for Children & Families
Alfred University
Saxon Drive
Alfred, NY 14802

Alfred University Press
ISBN Catalog Number: 0-9604962-4-6

Copies of *Play Therapy: A Do-It-Yourself Guide for Practitioners,* can be purchased from the Lea R. Powell Institute for Children and Families at Alfred University, Saxon Drive, Alfred, NY 14802.

Contact: Ellen Faherty, PsyD., (607) 871-2793
Email: faherty@alfred.edu

Acknowledgements

I would like to thank all those who have helped make this text a reality. My students in the Alfred University School Psychology Program and participants in the many workshops I have presented were essential in the development of the training model on which this book is based. Dr. Ellen Faherty provided invaluable suggestions and support as the editor of this work. Dr. Faherty and Dr. Edward Gaughan were critical in supporting the publication of this book by the Lea R. Powell Institute for Children and Families. Finally, special thanks to my wife, Wendy, and children, Caitlin, Ben, and Anna, who endured the many hours that I devoted to completing this book.

To all the children who taught me about the power of play.

Contents

Introduction vii

Chapter 1: Getting Started 1
What is Play Therapy?
Age Ranges
Choosing Your Toys
The Playroom
Play Session Self Assessment

Chapter 2: Therapeutic Responding ... 11
Introduction
Foundations of Responding
Rating the Type of Response with Adults
Identifying the Type of Response with Children
Response Practice
Homework
Play Session Self Assessment

Chapter 3: Limitsetting 23
Why Have Limits?
Approaches to Limitsetting
Common Limitsetting Pitfalls
Limitsetting Practice
Special Limitsetting Situations
The Truth About Limitsetting
Homework
Play Session Self Assessment

Chapter 4: Multicultural Issues in Play Therapy ... 39
Cultural Attitudes Pretest
Introduction
What is Culture?
The Between versus Within Group Differences Dilemma
Who Am I?
Multicultural Considerations in Play Therapy
Summary
Homework

Chapter 5: The First Session 49
Explaining the Reason for Referral
Orientation to the Counseling Situation
Discussing the Child's Likes and Dislikes
Obtaining Family Information
Giving the Child the Opportunity to Ask Questions
The Beginning of the First Play Therapy Session
A Word About General Pre-counseling Orientations
Homework

Chapter 6: Use of Games in Play Therapy ... 59
Homework
Play Session Self Assessment
Functions of Games
Typology of Games
Structure of Games
Cheating
Therapeutic Games
Summary
Homework
Play Session Self Assessment

Chapter 7: Therapist's Role 69
What is a Play Therapist?
A Matter of Attitude
Developing Your Creed
The Therapist's Role
Summary
Homework
Play Session Self Assessment

Chapter 8: Therapeutic Process 81
A General Process Model
Play Therapy Process Models
Research on Play Therapy Process
Summary
Homework

Chapter 9: Transferance and Countertransferance 89
What is Transferance?
Types of Transferance
Dealing with Transferance
Countertransferance: What Pushes Your Buttons?
Types of Countertransferance
Dealing with Countertransferance
Homework: Blindspots and Softspots

Chapter 10: Integrating Interventions 105
Play Therapy and a Concurrent Behavioral Intervention
Play Therapy and an Integrated Behavioral Intervention
A Metaphorical Storytelling Intervention
Summary
Homework: Storytelling Practice

Chapter 11: Termination 125
Determining if the Client is Ready to Terminate
Issues
The Termination Process
Homework: Termination Planning

Chapter 12: Orienting the Consumers 133
Counselor Goals
Instructional Objectives and Target Groups
Instructional Activities
Desired Outcomes
Workshop Materials

Chapter 13: Troubleshooting 151

References 155

Introduction

This book is designed for school and mental health professionals who are interested in using play therapy "today." As a practitioner of play therapy in school and clinical settings for many years and, later, as an educator of practitioners, I was struck by the lack of opportunities for training in this approach. Until recently, those of us who used play therapy were still basing our work on the guidelines provided by pioneers in the field 30 and 40 years ago (Axline, 1947; Moustakas, 1959; Schaefer & O'Connor, 1983). During the past ten years, play therapy has become one of the "buzzwords" in the helping professions, with new volumes being published (Donovan & McIntyre, 1990; Gil, 1991; Landreth, 1991; O'Connor, 1991) and a proliferation of introductory workshops. The drawback with this system of training is that, while books and workshops provide useful information about play therapy, they don't allow trainees to experience play therapy. The result is that after finishing a book or completing a workshop, practitioners feel they possess some knowledge about play therapy but lack the confidence to start using this approach because they haven't had the opportunity to assimilate their knowledge through experience.

The focus of this book is practical training in a general approach to play therapy. As the subtitle indicates, this is a "do-it-yourself" guide--a manual. A four stage self-instructional model is used (Figure 1). The purpose of breaking down training in this way is to allow trainees to gradually increase their comfort level with play therapy and confidence in their skills for using play therapy. This training process should allow the reader to initiate play therapy experiences, evaluate those experiences, and then seek feedback in the manual by referring to sections that address questions or issues that arise during the practice play sessions.

To support this approach to the use of this book, directions are given at the end of certain sections for the reader to engage in experiential activities before continuing on in the book. You should stop reading at those points and follow

Play Therapy Self-Instructional Model

Stage	Goal	Training Activities
1	Familiarization and comfort with common play materials.	Self play.
2	Development of basic micro-skills and conceptual foundation.	Observation of trainer and session videos. Simulations with adult partner. Exposure to different models.
3	Application of microskills and conceptual models.	Simulations with "practice" child.
4	Application and general skill development "in vivo."	Play therapy and supervision with real clients.

Figure 1

the directions for the "homework" assignment, as these activities are designed to bring the words on the page to life.

The practical emphasis of this manual also demands a different structure from other play therapy texts. The early chapters of the manual deal with the mechanics of using play therapy, including toy selection, room structure, responding, and limitsetting. It is my belief that knowledge follows experience. That is, a practitioner must begin using a technique or approach in order to understand the conceptual and theoretical underpinnings of the approach. In effect, experiencing a technique provides one with concrete examples for understanding concepts--it gives the trainee a "hook to hang a hat on." The later chapters of the book focus on the historical and theoretical frameworks of play therapy. The final section of the book provides ideas for educating professionals and parents about play therapy, and answers to common questions about the approach.

BASIC ASSUMPTIONS

Before beginning, it's important for you to know some of my basic assumptions about my work.

1. There's nothing new under the sun. The model that I am presenting here isn't new. It is an integration of play therapy approaches that have been used for decades. The model is simply the way I have learned to operate in my play therapy work over the years.
2. You can't be a one-horse show. Play therapy isn't the only approach you should use with children you see. But it is a good foundation approach. The model I use is an "open system" – that is, it provides a general framework within which I incorporate other techniques that will meet the specific needs of specific children.
3. One of the primary factors contributing to improvement in counseling is the counselor-client match. The development of a warm and caring relationship is critical to a "good match," and play therapy provides a natural medium through which the relationship can be developed with children.
4. The very nature of play makes play therapy an ideal approach for counseling children from culturally diverse populations. Play is universal: All children play! The form of the play and toys differ to some degree across cultures, but the fact that children play remains the same.
5. You can teach yourself this approach. While reading about play therapy and attending classes or workshops about play therapy will help you learn about play therapy, they won't help you learn play therapy. The best way to learn is through experience – by doing it and thinking about what you are doing. As Carl Whitaker said, "Nothing is worth learning that can't be experienced" (Whitaker & Bumberry, 1988).

This book provides a format for training yourself in play therapy. It is neither an introduction to the field of play therapy nor a summary of the research in this area. There already are many good references that provide this information (Landreth, 1991; O'Connor, 1991; Shaefer & O'Connor, 1983). I recommend that you read one of these texts to complement the training you will receive through this manual.

Chapter 1

Getting Started

What Is Play Therapy?

The term "play therapy" is usually used in reference to one of the many theoretical models for using play as a method of counseling children. Within this context, professionals typically have in mind a particular way of using play--that is, an underlying philosophical framework. In this manual, I am using the term play therapy generically, as I see the use of play media as a modality for counseling children, just as talking is a modality for counseling adults. Thus, I am not advocating any particular theoretical position on the use of play. Instead, this manual will focus on the microskills necessary for utilizing most play therapy approaches. These microskills include toy selection, therapeutic responding, therapeutic limitsetting, the use of games, and termination procedures.

As a point of reference, I'm going to try to define play therapy for you. I say "try" because play therapy is not just one approach, despite what you might read elsewhere. From my perspective, play therapy is many things, which I will outline below.

Play therapy is a modality. Play therapy is a counseling modality that incorporates the use of toys, art materials, games, and activities common to the experience of children. Through these activities children are able to communicate their feelings, thoughts, and needs, and counselors are able to develop an understanding of the internal experience of the child.

Play therapy is a method for approaching children on their level. When I counsel a child using play, I am in the child's territory. I am trying to see the world as the child sees it and understand the impact of the adult world on the child. Play is the child's most natural modus operandi, just as speaking is with adults.

Play therapy is a means for building a therapeutic relationship. Through the play therapy process, counselors establish the necessary relationship conditions which serve as the basis for therapeutic change (Rogers, 1957). Once these conditions are firmly established, change may occur either through direct intervention or the use of non-directive techniques.

Play therapy is a cluster of approaches that utilize play. There are many types of play therapies that offer counselors philosophical foundations on which to base their practice. There are four main groups of play therapies. Non-directive therapies focus more on relationship variables which enhance children's natural tendencies toward growth. Developmental play therapies are grounded in principles of child development and can be more directive and therapist-driven. Psychodynamic play therapies have descended from the earliest attempts to counsel children within a play framework and are rooted in psychoanalytic theory. Behavioral play therapies use play more for initial rapport-building and progress to more standard behavior modification techniques (O'Connor, 1991).

Play therapy is an attitude. The use of play as a counseling method assumes an underlying belief that play is an essential activity for children. Through play, children are behaving and interacting in a developmentally appropriate manner--practicing, modeling, communicating, and discharging feelings (Bettelheim, 1987; Erikson, 1963; Landreth, 1991). Thus, as a counselor, using play therapy is a way of conveying respect for the child's world and the belief that children are capable of using play effectively to deal with their internal experiences.

This certainly is not an all inclusive definition, and probably would not be one with which many of the experts in the field would necessarily agree. However, my view of play therapy is more cross-theoretical and focuses on client needs rather than adherence to a particular approach. As you progress in your self-instruction, consider this definition, and how you might revise it to create your own definition of play therapy.

AGE RANGES

Play therapy was originally developed for use with children ages three to six years old. Children younger than three are transitioning from the pre-language to the pre-operational stages of cognitive development, while children up to age six are firmly in the pre-operational stage (Piaget, 1962). Children in this stage are not able to use language abstractly, and, therefore, are not good candidates for traditional insight oriented talking therapy. Thus, play was viewed as a more natural, non-language based means for children to communicate their feelings and conflicts (Axline, 1947).

During the past 20 years, this view has broadened, and with it the age range in which play therapy is used. Even though children older than six years may be functioning above the pre-operational stage and able to use language more abstractly, play is still an important part of their everyday experience. Play is also a less direct avenue to children's internal lives (Erikson, 1963) and, therefore, a convenient means for circumventing defensiveness. Finally, play allows older children to regress to an earlier developmental level if they need to do this.

Nowadays, it is not unusual to see play therapy approaches used with older adolescents and young adults. The play activities chosen might be different from those used with younger children, but the underlying principles are still the same. The most typical age range for play therapy is ages three to eleven. However, I have worked with children as young as 18 months and as old as seventeen years using play techniques. My older clients who choose to play usually need to do so because of unmet needs related to an earlier stage of development. Once they trust me and know that I respect their need to regress, they spontaneously initiate the play therapy process. So, it is important to be open to the possibility that play therapy can be used beyond the pre-school or primary grade levels.

CHOOSING YOUR TOYS

GENERAL GUIDELINES FOR TOY SELECTION
Choosing to use play therapy usually dictates that toys will be needed when counseling a child. I say "usually" because there are some play therapy approaches--Theraplay comes to mind--that employ few, if any, toys. There are some general considerations when choosing toys.

Does the toy have therapeutic value? Every toy is not appropriate for a playroom. Toys should facilitate the therapeutic process in some way, such as enhancing emotional expression or allowing children to soothe themselves. Toys should also have the potential of being fun, but that should not be the only aspect considered.

Do the toys address a range of developmental levels? Since clients sometimes regress to an earlier developmental stage during play therapy, it is important to provide toys that are typically used by children at several different developmental levels. Thus, my playroom has toddler toys (music boxes, baby bottle), preschool toys (large blocks, dolls, finger paints), middle childhood toys (legos, paint, Nerf games, Trouble game), and late childhood toys (board games, therapeutic games). I recommend against trying to tailor the toy selection to one developmental level, particularly if you are working in a setting with somewhat older children. I once had an eleven-year-old, street smart boy as a client who immediately regressed in the play therapy situation and enjoyed playing with dolls and finger paints. Had I included only age-appropriate toys in the room, he would never have had that opportunity.

Toys should provide different levels of structure. While less structured media are traditionally preferred in play therapy, more structured purposeful toys do have a place in the playroom. Books and board games provide structure and distance that children sometimes need during the play therapy process. A mix of less structured and more structured toys allows clients to control the level of emotional closeness in the playroom until they become more comfortable with the therapeutic relationship.

Toys should offer opportunities for both individual and interactive play. The toys in the playroom should offer children the choice of playing by themselves or playing with the counselor. Most playroom media (art materials, legos) offer both possibilities while others (board games) serve one or the other purpose. This range of play opportunities is necessary because, as the play therapy process evolves, children often move from more self-centered play to relationship play in which they seek out interactions with the counselor.

TYPICAL PLAYROOM TOYS

Traditional approaches to play therapy--and my general approach falls in this category--require specific types of toys. Landreth (1987; 1991) classifies play therapy media into three primary groups: real-life, expressive, and aggressive/acting out. I add a fourth category--rule oriented toys. Examples of types of toys that fall within each group are provided in Figure 1-1 below.

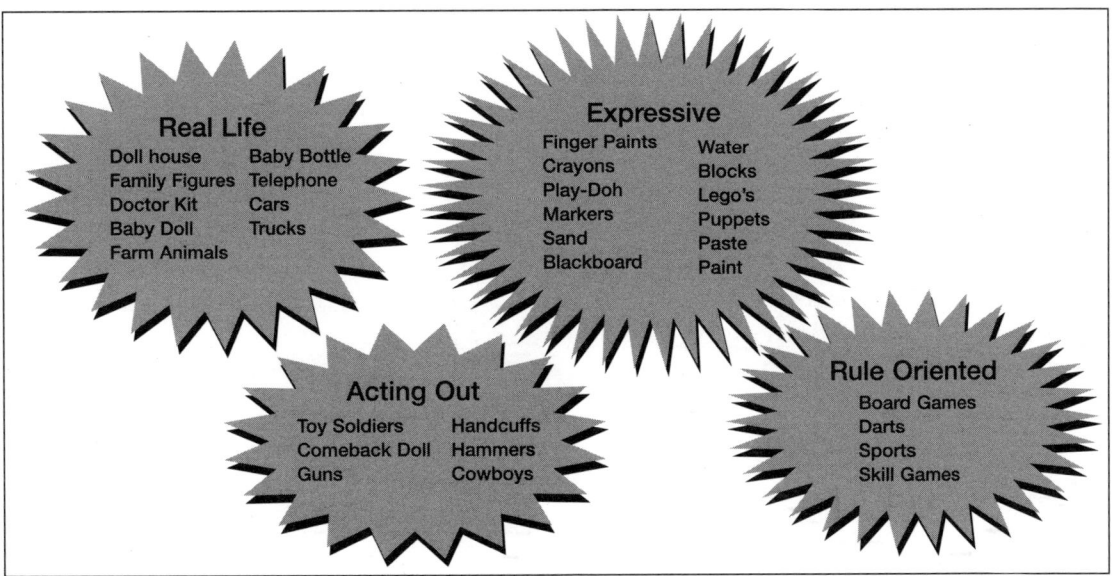

FIGURE 1-1 TOY SELECTION

Real-life Toys. Toys that comprise this category include such things as dollhouses, family figures, cars, cooking utensils, and the like--that is, things that are part of children's everyday experiences. The metaphors that can be developed using these toys also have a much closer relationship to reality. Thus, play involving family figures and a dollhouse usually has a direct relationship to interpersonal situations a child observes, or conflicts regarding relationships that a child may be experiencing. Real-life toys also provide templates for the practice and correcting of reality that is so much a part of children's play (Erikson, 1963). Some common uses of the real-life toys are discussed below.

Dollhouses and family figures are typically used to create play related to interpersonal and home situations. Baby dolls, baby bottles, cradles, and other types of baby toys are used in nurturing play (child taking care of doll) and acting out sibling conflicts (child acting out anger toward a new sibling). I have seen the telephone used most often as a way of communicating with the counselor without having to talk directly to him or her. A child will create a phone conversation with the counselor or a fantasy character and give the counselor an opportunity to respond to the child's conversation. This seems to provide a margin of safety for the child, particularly if the child is anxious about the counseling situation, or about disclosing information that might involve a parent or other significant person in the child's life. The doctor kit allows the child to undo or fix situations. For instance, if a child pretends to shoot the counselor, he or she might use the doctor's kit to make the counselor better, undoing the wrong. Cars are often used in play about traveling, in competitive play (racing), and in acting out play (crashing and destroying). Construction trucks are usually good to have available for sand play, and safety vehicles are often used in a similar way as the doctor's kit. Animals – farm, zoo, jungle – provide other media for interpersonal metaphors. Children who are not ready to use family figures to act out interpersonal conflicts will sometimes use animals for that purpose. This seems to remove the metaphor an additional step away from reality and make the play more emotionally safe for the child.

Expressive Media. Expressive media include art supplies, Play-Doh, sand, puppets, and building toys, like blocks. The main function of these types of toys is to provide less structured ways of expressing and discharging emotions. With this type of media, children can choose how directly related to reality their productions will be. For instance, a child might paint a picture that clearly depicts a real-life experience about which he/she is experiencing conflicts. Or, a child may simply make a multi-colored blob of clay and call it "the evil monster." Art media are traditionally seen as allowing individuals to express feelings more abstractly. Puppets, on the other hand, provide props for expressing feelings through role plays. Sand and blackboards allow children to create things and then erase them, leaving no permanent product. Construction toys serve a similar purpose.

Acting Out Toys. Acting out toys typically include things like hammers, guns, and handcuffs; action figures like soldiers, cowboys, and pirates; and the bobo or comeback doll, an air-inflated punching doll that returns to an upright position after being knocked over. The purpose of acting out toys is to allow children to express anger and release aggressive feelings. The type of release may be general, such as simply banging on a wooden workbench with a hammer or randomly hitting the bobo; or quite specific, such as pretending to shoot the father doll.

These toys are often used for other purposes in addition to expressing anger. For instance, some children will handcuff me when playing a game of Nerf basketball in order to "level the playing field;" that is, to insure that our potential skill levels are equivalent. In this case the handcuffs are a way that the child expresses some doubts about his or her ability and exerts some control in compensating for these doubts. Action figures are commonly used to play out situations of protection, a child arranging the figures around another figure to serve as defenders. The point to keep in mind is that even though we, the adults, have these toys available for certain purposes, children will tailor the use of the toys to their needs.

Inclusion of guns in play therapy is a controversial topic. If a toy gun is not available, children will use their fingers or such things as blocks for guns. For most children, the use of guns is not a sign of violent tendencies. Children engage in play involving guns whether toy guns are available or not--this is a developmental phenomenon that appears around age four. It is a type of power-and-control play and/or a way a child expresses anger (Bettelheim, 1987). I have conducted play therapy both with and without guns present in the playroom, and have finally settled on including more fantasy-based guns, such as cowboy guns. If you work in a setting where guns are not allowed or you are uncomfortable with providing toy guns, then you should not include guns with your toys. Many play therapists establish rules about the use of toy guns, examples of which are described in Chapter Three.

Prescribing such behaviors as hitting the bobo or a pillow as a means of reducing aggressive tendencies is not a good practice. There is a substantial body of research in the social learning field that demonstrates that encouraging such behavior actually increases the frequency of aggressive behavior (Bandura, 1973). When children hit the bobo or bang on a table with a hammer spontaneously, their behavior is being generated internally, something Oaklander (1992) has labeled "aggressive energy." Thus, they are using the play as an outlet for their feelings. When children are told to hit something, their behavior is being generated by an external stimulus (an adult), and, in a sense, this directive gives children permission to be aggressive. Landreth (1991) recommends including egg cartons in the playroom as an outlet for anger. He allows clients to destroy the egg cartons and sees this as a useful alternative for children who want to bang or throw toys.

Rule-Oriented Toys. The use of games in play therapy is not generally accepted. Traditional non-directive therapists see games as non-facilitative and non-therapeutic (Landreth). They cite the competitive elements, rule-orientation, and structure of most common children's games as factors which interfere with children's creativity and flexibility in expressing themselves. Despite these objections, the fact of the matter is that games are common elements of most children's experience. Thus, eclectic and psychodynamically oriented therapists use games as a means of assessing underlying issues and the dynamics of the counselor-client relationship (Schaefer & Reid, 1986).

A few simple guidelines should be considered when choosing games. First, games should be relatively common or available in the child's everyday experience (home, school, friend's houses). Second, games should facilitate counselor-client interactions. Since computer games tend to absorb most of a child's focus, they do not meet this second criteria. Third, the rules of the game should be easy to understand. Fourth, the game should be one in which an adult and child have an approximately equal chance of winning. Finally, the range of games selected should include games that rely primarily on luck to games that require a certain level of skill. The purpose of this will be discussed on the next page.

There are certain games that meet the above criteria which are commonly included in play resources. These games are listed in Figure 1-2.

As mentioned above, each of these games falls on a continuum of luck to skill. In Candyland, a game in which players draw cards that determine the number of spaces they move,

FIGURE 1-2 GAMES

progress depends on the luck of the draw. In Sorry, cards are also drawn that determine the number of spaces moved, but a certain amount of strategy is required to win. For instance, there are cards on which a choice must be made about the type of move, number of spaces, or dividing the move between two pieces. In Monopoly, luck is involved in the role of the dice, but there is a substantial amount of skill required in deciding what properties to buy and sell.

So, how are games helpful in play therapy? I find games useful in the following ways. First, games allow the counselor to assess where a child is functioning developmentally in dealing with competition and rules. During middle childhood (ages 9-12) children become interested in rule-oriented play. This is part of the process of developing moral decision-making skills and an understanding of cause-effect. Children who shy away from these types of activities or who are easily discouraged during the course of a game may be dealing with issues that interfere with this developmental process, such as low frustration tolerance and low self esteem.

Because of this, games provide opportunities for observing children's frustration tolerance and self esteem. Children who immediately want to stop playing games when they fall behind often find losing so damaging to their sense of self that they cannot tolerate even the possibility that they won't win. For these children, the use of games needs to involve a gradual building up of frustration tolerance through specific interventions. This type of intervention might progress through the following sequence: 1) The counselor deliberately loses to the child and models coping skills through externalized self talk; 2) The counselor gradually allows the outcome of games to get closer and closer, all the while continuing to model coping strategies for the increased level of frustration, and simultaneously reinforcing clients' uses of these strategies when they become upset by the closeness of the game; and 3) The counselor begins playing the game normally and reinforcing clients' appropriate responses to losing.

Because of the structured nature of games, they provide opportunities for children to act out aggression and anger toward adults in a safe and contained way. Thus, the child who is mad at a teacher might send the counselor's game pieces back to "start" in Trouble whenever the opportunity presents itself (and with a great deal of glee). In this way, games provide an excellent template for children to act out transference and, because of the structure, keep these interactions relatively contained and safe for clients.

Games also provide a means for children to "pull back" at times when the intensity of the therapy is overwhelming. Again, the structure of games helps the child to maintain contact with the counselor while decreasing the level of emotional stimulation. This allows clients to recoup their internal resources and then return to other play activities when they are ready.

Many counselors include only therapeutic games in their toys because of the non-competitive and educational nature of these games. I do include these types of games and find them useful with older children who are at an impasse in counseling, with activity groups, and as interventions for specific problems (e.g., social skills deficits). My objection to the exclusive use of therapeutic games is that they are not common to children's experience. Thus, by restricting my clients to therapeutic games, I am forcing my adult perspective on them.

Reading Materials. Reading materials such as books and self-help manuals for children are not play media per se; thus, more traditional play therapists sometimes view them as inappropriate for inclusion in the playroom. Reading materials are used for the counseling approaches that have been labeled bibliotherapies, where the primary therapeutic activity involves readings that are related to the child's problem. However, I have found that children use books in play therapy when it fits their needs. In some cases, books serve a function similar to games, a child moving to a book to reduce anxiety and recoup resources after a particularly intense play segment.

Reading materials may also be used as bibliotherapy when the child seeks out a book that is related to his or her problem. I have found that reading provides opportunities for intimacy and affection between a child and me in situations where the child seeks out quiet time by having me read a book with him or her.

In selecting reading materials, you want to meet the needs of a wide developmental range and provide materials on a broad range of topics. General readings include such materials as Golden Books and the Berenstein Bears for younger children, and books by authors such as Judy Blume and Beverly Cleary for latency age children. Issue-specific materials include books on divorce, alcoholism, child abuse, ADHD, death, relocation, and peer problems.

Keep in mind that a child's choice of a general versus an issue type book does not automatically mean that the child is not experiencing a conflict in a particular area. Even traditional fairy tales may have meaning for a child. "The Three Little Pigs" became a favorite for a boy I once saw whose father was continually threatening to hurt the boy's mother. Because it was too threatening for the boy to read a book that dealt directly with the fear he experienced related to domestic abuse, the fairy tale provided him with the distance he needed. On the other hand, a child may just randomly pick a title in order to have time to sit and read with the counselor, as a way of connecting with him or her. Having both types of reading materials available allows children the choice of how directly they want to deal with their emotional conflict.

TIPS FOR ACQUIRING TOYS

Toys can be obtained from a number of sources. In collecting your playroom materials, keep the guidelines provided above in mind. *Don't* select a toy simply because it looks like it would be fun. The toys you select need to have a therapeutic purpose for being in your playroom.

Keeping this in mind, garage/yard/rummage

sales are good sources of used toys. You can often obtain early childhood toys, dollhouses, dolls, and some of the traditional games mentioned above from these sales. Toy departments of large discount stores and large toy stores, particularly superstores, are also excellent sources for basic play therapy toys. If you work in a school, the art teacher is an important friend. Art supplies such as finger paints, tempera paints, markers, crayons, paste, and the like should be available from the art teacher. This will help keep your supply costs down considerably.

If you are working in a limited space or are itinerant, you will want your toys to be small enough to be portable or to fit in a small space. Therefore, you should choose smaller versions of the toys listed above. For instance, instead of buying a barrel of Legos, just buy a small starter kit. Instead of large rubber animals, use the smaller plastic ones. While it is nice to have a large sand table or floor sandbox in the playroom, this is often not possible in an office that has multiple uses. A rectangular plastic storage container serves the same purpose and fits easily on a table. If the most important person in your professional life--your building custodian--does not like the mess associated with using sand, then rice, oatmeal, small glass aquarium beads, and the like can be just as useful, although somewhat more limited in terms of building structures. The same principle applies to dollhouses. It's nice to have a large wooden dollhouse, but not always practical. There are a number of good fold out plastic dollhouses on the market that meet this need, are portable, and fit in limited spaces.

Bobo dolls are now much more available than in years past. The typical vinyl blow-up doll ($4.00 to $7.00 range) is adequate, although not sturdy enough to be jumped on or punched hard by an older child. There are therapeutic bobo dolls on the market that are ruggedly constructed and have lifetime guarantees, but are quite expensive ($90.00-$160.00 range). If you don't have floor space for a bobo, a hanging blow-up toy can serve the same purpose.

THE PLAYROOM

Playrooms come in all shapes and sizes. In fact, it was only recently that I worked in a facility where I had a designated playroom. Otherwise, the "playroom" has always been an area of my office. So, it is probably more accurate to talk about "play spaces" rather than playrooms. During the course of my career, I have done play therapy in book storage rooms, the stage of a cafetorium (curtains closed, of course), closet-size offices, medium-size offices, and in large offices that provided considerable space for play therapy. In each situation, I had to adapt the play therapy to my space while preserving the basics of the approach.

Child-size Furniture: Whenever possible, use tables and chairs that are designed for children. Smaller tables and chairs bring the counselor down to the child's level and, thus, allow you to develop a better sense of how the child perceives the world.

If you work in a school setting, child furniture is usually readily available. I used trapezoid or semi-circular tables in my office because these could be conveniently pushed together to make a larger table for groups. I would set the table height to make it comfortable for children sitting in chairs that were used in second and third grade classrooms.

If you don't work in a school, affordable child furniture can be purchased through such outlets as IKEA and Service Merchandise. Furniture is also available through toy superstores such as Toys R Us, but is usually higher priced. As with toys, garage sales are also sources of useful items. If you are in a situation in which having child furniture is not possible, just make sure that the chairs allow children to reach the table top easily.

Floor Spaces. It is nice to provide both carpeted and uncarpeted floor space in your play area. Carpeted areas are more user friendly for floor and rough-and-tumble play. Uncarpeted areas are good for messy items, such as paints, sand, Play-Doh and water.

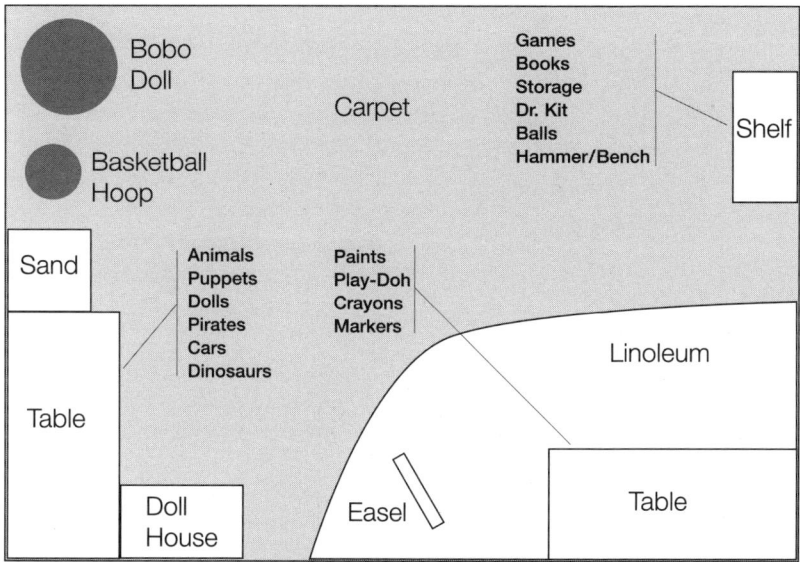

FIGURE 1-3 PLAYROOM SET-UP

Setting up floor space is fairly simple. If you are in an office that has only uncarpeted floor, an inexpensive throw rug or end piece of carpeting can provide your alternative space. The size of the rug should be determined by the space with which you are working. If you are in a carpeted office, a grease cloth or plastic rug protector that is used under desk chairs will provide adequate protection for the carpet in the "messy media" area. Figure 1-3 provides a sample floor plan of a play area.

Predictability. The important thing about the play space isn't the size or the layout. It is PREDICTABILITY. What makes the play therapy situation different from other situations for clients is the predictability and stability of the situation. In order for the therapeutic environment to be effective, children need to know what to expect when they enter the playroom.

The play space is the concrete manifestation of this predictability. Everything in the playroom has its place and that place is always the same. Thus, toys and furniture are always set up the same way at the beginning of each play session. How things are arranged depends on the space available. Toys can be on shelves or displayed on tables. Larger items such as sand trays and dollhouses can be on tables or the floor. The important thing to keep in mind is the consistency of arrangement.

I typically arrange my play area in the following way. Art materials are on a separate table or a designated section of a large table. If I have a small dollhouse, I will also place that on a table top or stand. I usually keep large dollhouses on the floor. Family dolls are placed next to or in front of the dollhouses. Many of the real life toys are placed on a shelf or on a section of a large table separate from the expressive media. Games and books are also on a shelf. Sand trays are placed on the floor or a child-size stand. Blocks and the bobo doll are placed on the floor.

HOMEWORK ASSIGNMENT
You should stop reading and take time to purchase toys and set up a play area in your office or home to begin practicing. Your first assignment is to play three times by yourself with all the toys in the play area, a minimum of 30 minutes per session. Complete the activity sheet on the next page after your third session.

PLAY SESSION SELF ASSESSMENT

1. With which toys did you feel most comfortable? Why?

2. With which toys did you feel most uncomfortable? Why?

3. Did you experience any particular thoughts in relation to certain play activities (memories, visualizations, etc.)?

    Play Activity   Thought

4. Did you experience any strong feelings in relation to certain play activities?

    Play Activity   Feeling

5. List any questions you have about play therapy at this point.

Continue on to the next chapter.

Chapter 2

Therapeutic Responding

What Is a Facilitative Response?

Experts in the play therapy field offer many perspectives on what constitutes a "good" counselor response to a client's play behavior (Landreth, 1991; O'Connor & Braverman, 1997). Unfortunately, their ideas are based primarily on their theoretical framework rather than any type of research on microskills in play therapy. A non-directive or humanistic play therapist will identify reflective responses as "good" and interpretive responses as "bad," while a psychodynamic play therapist sees interpretive responses as being "good." Thus, the types of counselor responses that have been identified as appropriate reflect the philosophical viewpoint of the expert.

In my cross-theoretical approach to play therapy, I tend to rely on the substantial body of microskills research with adults produced by Carkhuff, Truax, Berenson, and Ivey (Carkhuff & Berenson, 1977; Ivey & Ivey, 1999; Truax & Carkhuff, 1967). This research has identified behaviors that tend to facilitate client communication in counseling. While the research is generic, it does support the earlier research and principles of the Person-Centered approach developed by Carl Rogers (Rogers, 1961). My ideas regarding effective responding are downward extrapolations of this research. Hence, I am biased toward the more non-directive type of responding, at least during the early stages of the therapeutic process.

Foundations of Responding

Non-Verbal Cues. Arnold Mehrabian (1971) conducted a classic study in which he examined the effects of verbal and non-verbal communication on accurate identification of emotions. From this study he proposed the following formula:

Total Feeling = 7% Verbal + 38% Vocal + 55% Facial

In other words, the actual exchange of words provided the least important cues regarding how people were feeling. Vocal intonation was much more important, and facial expression the most important factor in accurate identification of feelings.

This is a critical idea to understand when using play to counsel children. As children play, they may or may not be talking. However, even if they are talking, this comprises only a small portion of the message. What they are doing – their non-verbal cues and reactions in play – are much more important to the counselor's understanding. So, when I am responding to children, I am responding to their actions as much or more than I am to their verbalizations.

Attending Behaviors. Gerard Egan (1994) has taken the research on attending skills and formulated a general model for facilitative behavior in adult counseling situations, which he summarizes in the acronym, "SOLER:"

S	=	Face the client squarely
O	=	Open posture
L	=	Lean toward the client
E	=	Make eye contact
R	=	Relax

These behaviors are ones that have been shown to increase verbal output, and, thus, are seen as facilitative when conducting talking therapy with adults.

In play therapy, these attending behaviors can be extrapolated downward and defined as behaviors which communicate interest in and attention to what children are doing as they play. I define these behaviors in the nonsensical acronym, S-K-I-L-L-E-D.

S = SIT in close proximity to the child, while allowing the child to determine the comfort zone.

K = Place yourself physically on the KID'S level.

I = Show INTEREST by giving your undivided attention.

L = LOOK at what the child is doing.

L = LISTEN to what the child is saying.

E = Convey EMPATHY for the child.

D = DESCRIBE what you're seeing as well as hearing.

Since sitting squarely is not always possible as a child plays, sitting relatively close to where the child is playing serves the same purpose. Placing myself on the child's level helps me engage a child, just as eye contact and open posture does with adults. Showing interest by describing what the child is doing is analogous to leaning toward an adult who is disclosing information verbally in a counseling situation. Observing and listening to the child are keys to understanding the child's frame of reference and, thereby, developing empathy for the child. Describing what the child is doing through facilitative responses is the means of conveying empathy to the child.

Facilitative Conditions. In addition to attending behaviors, there is a cluster of therapeutic conditions that have been identified as enhancing the therapeutic relationship. These conditions, first proposed by Carl Rogers (1957), have been shown to be critical predictors of positive therapeutic outcomes in some 50 plus years of clinical research (Lambert & Bergin, 1994). My good friends and mentors, Dr. Hugh Gunnison (a.k.a. Gunner) and Dr. T.F. Renick (a.k.a. Fritz), labeled these conditions the PEGS (Gunnison, 1999):

P = Unconditional Positive Regard
E = EMPATHY
G = Genuineness
S = Specificity of Response

I find this to be a handy acronym for remembering the conditions--the PEGS that hold the counseling relationship together.

I capitalized empathy because this variable has been shown to be critical to therapeutic progress *across counseling approaches*. Even if you are using a strict behavioral intervention, you need to develop and convey a sense of empathy to the client if you are going to be effective as a therapist. I see this as extremely important when working with children because our adult frames of reference are so different from those of kids. In order to understand what a child is going through, I need to develop empathy for that child. And the way I can do this is by crawling into the child's world on his or her own level. Play becomes the vehicle for doing this.

Facilitative responding is the means for conveying these facilitative conditions. In this type of responding, the counselor is giving the child his or her *undivided* attention and is conveying interest in and understanding of what the child is doing. The counselor needs to do this both non-verbally (getting down on the child's level, watching the child) and verbally (describing the play, labeling feelings that are observed). The SKILLED framework provides guidelines for basic descriptive responses. In addition to describing what the child is doing, the counselor should also pay attention to and label feelings that are being expressed through the play. Tips for responding are contained in Figure 2-1.

PEGS:
Communicate acceptance, and warmth. Be "real" in reactions to child's play.

Questions:
When absolutely necessary. . .
- to explain a behavior the therapist does not understand.
- in the intervention stage when appropriate.

Responsibility:
Responses should encourage responsibility and initiative.

Interpretation:
DON'T! This imposes your frame of reference.

KISS:
Keep it Short and Simple (and interactive)

Personalize:
Respond as you would to an adult – in the second person. Don't use the third person or "we."

Metaphors:
Stay within the child's symbol system.

FIGURE 2-1 RESPONSE TIPS

RATING THE TYPE OF RESPONSE WITH ADULTS

Truax and Carkhuff (1967) and Carkhuff and Berenson (1977) conducted considerable research on the types of responses that are most effective when counseling adults. This research led to the development of a typology of facilitative effectiveness of responses. This typology or rating format is summarized in Figure 2-2.

Level	Conveys
1	No Understanding/No Direction
2	No Understanding/Some Direction
3	Understanding/No Direction
4	Understanding/Some Direction
5	Deep Understanding/Clear Direction

FIGURE 2-2 CARKHUFF & BERENSON RESPONSE RATINGS

A Level 1 response is one that completely misses the mark in terms of understanding. For example, a crying child comes in to the counselor at the beginning of the school day and says, "My dog got killed last night." The counselor replies, "Aren't you Jimmy Smith's brother?" This response has no connection to the child's message or feeling, conveying general disinterest to the child. Thus, the response conveys no understanding and no direction about what the child should do next. An example of a Level 2 response might be, "You can always get another dog." In this case, the counselor provides specific direction, but again shows no understanding of the child's grief. Level 1 and 2 responses are also called subtractive responses (Sydnor, Akridge, & Parkhill, 1972), as these types of responses tend to interfere with (or subtract from) the counseling relationship.

The lowest level facilitative response is a Level 3 response. A Level 3 response in the above scenario would be, "I can see that you are very sad." In this example, the counselor conveyed understanding of the child's plight but provided no direction regarding what to do next. This type of response is sometimes referred to as an interchangeable response because it basically reflects the client's feeling or comments. Effective counselors use this type of response most often during the early and middle stages of the counseling process when clients are exploring and developing understanding of issues (Carkhuff & Berenson, 1977).

The highest levels of facilitative responses are Level 4 and 5 responses. These types of responses are most commonly found in the later or action stage of the counseling process when clients are developing strategies for addressing issues they have identified. Thus, in the present child scenario, a Level 4 response might be, "I can see you are very sad. You can sit with me for a while and talk a little more or just have quiet time if you want." These statements let the child know that the counselor is listening and provide some direction concerning what the child might do next. Level 5 responses would come later, perhaps after three or four sessions or more, as the child moves through the bereavement process. An example of a Level 5 response might be, "It's obvious that you are still very sad and don't just want to forget your dog. What are some things you could do to remember your dog?" The difference between Level 4 and Level 5 responses is more degree than form. In these examples, both responses show understanding and provide direction, but the Level 5 is more specific (Carkhuff & Berenson, 1977). These types of responses are called additive responses because they facilitate or add to the counseling process (Sydnor et al., 1972).

Just for practice, try rating the sample responses at right. Compare your ratings to the answers at the bottom of the page when you are finished.

Rating	Response
_____	**Client:** My boss just sat there in front of all those people and made me feel stupid--like I was a two-year-old. **Counselor:** *Sounds like you felt demeaned and hurt.*
_____	**Client:** It's unbelievable. I actually won the scholarship. It's like the beginning of a whole new life. **Counselor:** *It's one of those pleasant shocks. Now you can start thinking about all the possibilities this opens up.*
_____	**Client:** The next thing I knew, he was hitting me. My husband was hitting me. **Counselor:** *Did your husband finish high school?*
_____	**Client:** It just doesn't seem fair. Some people get all the breaks in life...and I get all the crap. **Counselor:** *Well, you'll just have to pull yourself up by the bootstraps.*
_____	**Client:** So, I know now that it's time to move on. I'm ready for a challenge and this job is no longer for me. **Counselor:** *Sounds like, deep down inside you're ready for a change. Maybe this is a good time to discuss the types of careers you have been daydreaming about, now that you've made a decision.*

Answers: 3, 4, 1, 2, 5.

IDENTIFYING THE TYPE OF RESPONSE WITH CHILDREN

Unfortunately, there is no similar research-based system for rating responses used in child counseling in general, and play therapy in particular. Landreth (1991) provides excellent and extensive guidelines for responding facilitatively in play therapy, but his analysis of what constitutes an appropriate response is based largely on his theoretical/philosophical orientation. I can offer no more than he in terms of research support, but I will attempt to provide a more general framework for analyzing whether or not a response is facilitative.

My response typology is based on a few simple assumptions. First, my experience has taught me that there is a range of appropriate facilitative responses. When counseling children, it is more important to be accurate and show a child that you are within the ballpark of understanding, than to be precise and pick the one best response possible. Second, children are fairly open and willing to give counselors immediate feedback regarding whether or not their responses were accurate. The feedback may be verbal, such as telling counselors outright that they are wrong, or non-verbal, such as withdrawing or making a sudden change in play activity. Third, most children are relatively resilient. Hence, one particular inaccurate response by a counselor neither destroys the relationship nor the child.

Given these assumptions, the way I think about facilitative responses in play therapy is based more on the function of facilitative responses rather than a rating of effectiveness. Thus, I first classify responses as either facilitative or non-facilitative. I then subdivide facilitative play therapy responses into four categories. This classification scheme and its relationship to the counseling process is illustrated in Figure 2-3.

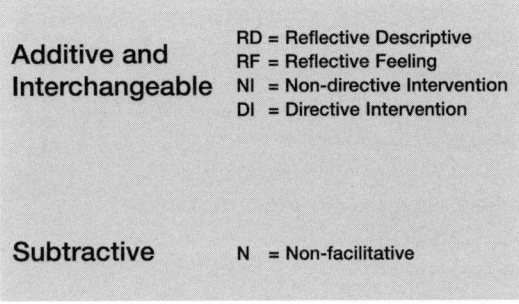

FIGURE 2-3 FACILITATIVE RESPONSES IN PLAY THERAPY

Reflective Descriptive (RD) responses are straightforward feedback to the child regarding his or her observable behavior.

EXAMPLE:
Client Behavior: Child is having two dolls fight.

Counselor Response: Those dolls are really hitting each other.

The purpose of this type of response is to communicate to the child that you are paying attention to and understanding his/her play.

In a Reflective Feeling (RF) response, the counselor focuses on the emotion that is evident in the child's play and labels it.

EXAMPLE:
Client Behavior: Child is having two dolls fight.

Counselor Response: It looks like that doll is really mad at that one.

The purpose of this type of response is to help children become aware of their feelings and to provide the opportunity to discharge these feelings and feel understood.

The purpose of Non-directive Intervention (NI) and Directive Intervention (DI) responses is to aid the child in problem-solving and the development of coping strategies, and/or to help the child attain closure on an issue. These responses are more action oriented and, as indicated by the labels, may be open-ended or quite specific.

EXAMPLE:
Client Behavior: Child is having two dolls fight that she identifies as the mother and father, and has a doll identified as the daughter watching.

Counselor NI Response: It looks like the parents are really mad at each other. What is something the daughter could do?

Client: The daughter could get in between them and stop them.

Counselor DI Response: That wouldn't be very safe for the daughter. What is something the daughter could do that would be safe.

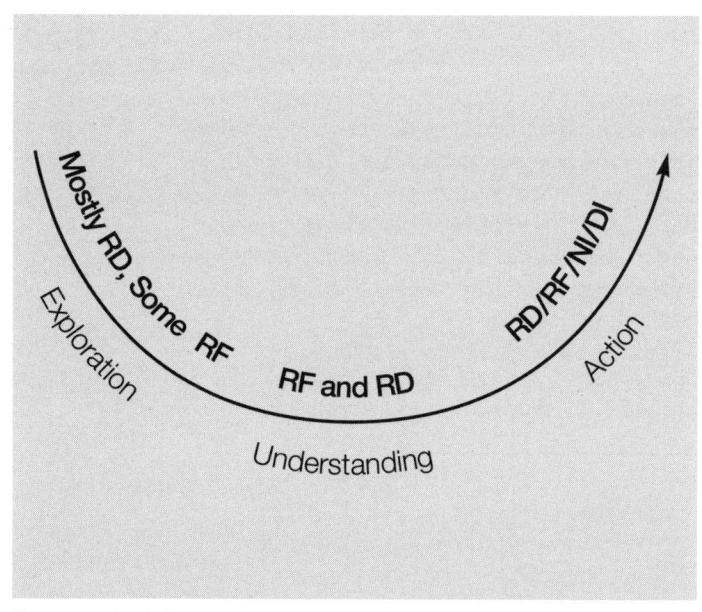

FIGURE 2-4 RESPONSES IN THE PLAY THERAPY PROCESS

Certain types of responses are more characteristic of specific stages of the counseling process (Figure 2-4). I tend to use RD and RF responses more during the beginning and middle stages of counseling, as I see these as generally facilitating more exploration and understanding of issues. NI and DI responses are used more in the action phase of counseling when the client is problem-solving and closing out issues. However, it is important to keep in mind that counseling is not a lock-step activity, thus, any of these responses may be appropriate in any stage of counseling. I am only attempting to provide a conceptual scheme for what has seemed most typical to me across the many of clients I have seen.

RESPONSE PRACTICE

At this point, it is time to practice some basic responding skills to begin developing the mind set of responding in different ways to children's play. For each of the following vignettes, cover the suggested responses and formulate your own descriptive (RD) and feeling (RF) responses to the situation. Then compare your responses to the suggested responses that are provided. Remember, there is a range of appropriate responses, the suggested responses simply provide some idea of possible responses that might be used in each situation. After completing this exercise, go on to Chapter 3.

PRACTICE VIGNETTES

Directions: Read each vignette and decide how you might respond if you were working with the child. Sample responses are provided.

1. Child enters room, sits down, and stares at the table for several minutes after you have introduced her to the playroom.

   RD Responses:
   Looks like you just want to sit there.
   Looks like you don't want to do anything right now.
   Looks like you aren't ready to start just yet.
   Looks like you are *choosing* not to play right now.
   RF Responses:
   Seems like you don't *feel* like doing anything just yet.

2. Child enters the room and sits quietly for several minutes looking around the room after you have introduced him to the playroom.

   Your Responses:

   RD: _____

   _____

   _____

   RF: _____

   _____

   _____

Suggested Responses:
   RD:
   Looks like you're just checking things out.
   Looks like you are trying to *decide* where to start.
   RF:
   Looks like you aren't *sure* where to begin (or what to begin with).

3. Child enters the room and goes from toy to toy, playing just a few seconds and then moving on to the next toy.
Your Responses:

RD: _____

_____

_____

RF: _____

_____

_____

Suggested Responses:
RD:
Seems like you are trying to play with a lot of things (or everything).
You are trying lots of things out today.
RF:
You seem really *curious* about the toys here.

---

4. Child is banging on the play house with a hammer and finally tips the house over.
Your Responses:

RD: _____

_____

_____

RF: _____

_____

_____

Suggested Responses:
RD:
You are really banging on that house a lot (or hard, etc.).
Looks like you *need* to wreck (break, bang on) that house.
RF:
Looks like you are really *angry* [about _____].
Seems like you are *frustrated*.

5. Child is pretending to have a stuffed dog attack other stuffed animals.
   Your Responses:

   RD: _____

   _____

   _____

   RF: _____

   _____

   _____

Suggested Responses:
   RD:
   It's fighting with the other animals.
   Looks like it's trying to bite (attack, etc.) the other animals (or "them").
   RF:
   Looks like it's really *mad* at the other animals (or "them").

6. Child makes dinosaurs out of Play-Doh and then says, "This is the mommy dinosaur, this is the daddy dinosaur, and this is the baby dinosaur. The daddy dinosaur is hitting the mommy. [Child picks up scissors.] So Scissor Man comes and cuts daddy dinosaur's head off."
   Your Responses:

   RD: _____

   _____

   _____

   RF: _____

   _____

   _____

Suggested Responses:
   RD:
   Scissor Man cut that daddy dinosaur's head off.
   Scissor Man is trying to stop the daddy dinosaur from hurting the mommy.
   Looks like Scissor Man is protecting the mommy and the baby dinosaurs.
   RF:
   Scissor Man is very, very *mad* at the daddy dinosaur.
   Scissor Man wants to *punish* the daddy dinosaur.

7. Child begins to crawl around on the floor, talks baby talk, and asks you to hold a baby bottle so he can nurse.
   Your Responses:

   RD: _____

   _____

   _____

   RF: _____

   _____

   Suggested Responses:
   RD: Looks like you need to be a baby right now.
         You're crawling and talking and eating just like a baby.
   RF: You feel like it would be nice to be taken care of like a baby.

8. Child uses blocks to build a wall between you and her. She tells you to stay on the other side of the wall.
   Your Responses:

   RD: _____

   _____

   _____

   RF: _____

   _____

   Suggested Responses:
   RD: You want me to stay over here.
         Looks like you made that wall to keep us apart.
         You worked very hard to build that wall in front of you.
   RF: Looks like you need to have your own space.
         Maybe it makes you feel safe to have that wall between us.
         It looks like you want to protect yourself with that wall.

Chapter Two: Therapeutic Responding   **21**

9. Child cleans and organizes the playroom for most of the session.
   Your Responses:

   RD: _____

   _____

   _____

   RF: _____

   _____

   Suggested Responses:
   RD: You really need to have everything just right.
         You are getting everything organized here.
         You're making sure that the room is set up just the way you want it.
   RF: It seems like you don't like any kind of mess.
         You feel better when things are clean and orderly.
         It seems like you get upset when the room isn't the way you want it.

10. Child makes three houses out of sand in the sandbox. Then, pointing to each house, she says, "This is the father bear's house, and this is the mother bear's house, and this is the baby bear's house. The baby bear doesn't want to live with the mother or father anymore."

    Your Responses:

    RD: _____

    _____

    _____

    RF: _____

    _____

    Suggested Responses:
    RD:
    So they each have their own houses.
    They aren't going to live together now.
    The baby doesn't want to live with the mother and father bears anymore.
    RF:
    The baby bear must be mad at the mother and father bears.
    The baby bear doesn't like living with the mother and father bears right now.
    The baby bear is upset with its parents.
    The baby bear has decided that it would be better off (or happier) living alone.

Homework Assignment

It is time to begin practicing the basic responding skills. You should begin doing this by practicing in simulated play therapy sessions. You will need to find an adult partner--a friend, colleague, spouse, etc.--who will be the "child" during the session. Then, choose one of the role play situations provided below. Your partner will need to simulate behaviors of the child client that he/she is role playing. Your task is to respond to the client's play using the facilitative responses described above. Your client should try as much as possible to play and not talk as adults tend to do. After completing two different simulations, complete the self-evaluation form at the end of this chapter.

Simulation Roles

Client 1:
Five-year-old who wants to play house, baby, etc.

Client 2:
Five-year-old who likes to play rough-and-tumble games like cowboys, cops-and-robbers, etc.

Client 3:
Seven-year-old who wants to take care of and please the therapist.

Client 4:
Seven-year-old who was severely physically abused by his mother. Play focuses on safety themes.

Client 5:
Eight-year-old who needs to regress and pretend to be an infant, toddler, and pre-schooler.

Client 6:
Anxious nine-year-old who needs to keep everything neat.

PLAY SESSION SELF ASSESSMENT

1. With which toys did you feel most comfortable? Why?

2. With which toys did you feel most uncomfortable? Why?

3. Did you experience any particular thoughts in relation to certain play activities (memories, visualizations, etc.)?

   Play Activity					Thought

4. Did you experience any strong feelings in relation to certain play activities?

   Play Activity					Feeling

5. List any questions you have about play therapy at this point.

Continue on to the next chapter.

Chapter 3

Limitsetting

Why Have Limits in the Playroom?

Limitsetting is one of the thorny procedures in play therapy, and one with which novice therapists typically struggle. But limits are a necessity of the playroom structure that help make the playroom setting predictable and safe. Without a sense of structure in the playroom, children are forced to guess about the appropriateness of their play behaviors, potentially and unnecessarily increasing their anxiety and placing them at risk of becoming overstimulated, out of control, or emotionally overexposed.

The primary reason for establishing limits in the playroom is to provide structure and predictability. It is important for kids to have a sense of what they can and cannot do, what toys are available to them, how they go about playing, how much time they have, and what areas are off limits in the playroom or office. In addition, limits are necessary for insuring the emotional and physical safety of the child, the physical safety of the counselor, the condition of the play area, and the integrity of the counseling relationship (Landreth, 1991). Specifically, children need to know that it is okay to be upset in the playroom, but it is not okay to start hitting themselves or the counselor. They need to understand that they can do almost anything that isn't dangerous with the toys, but they aren't allowed to damage a toy or the playroom. They can have fun and make messes, but they can't purposely mess up themselves or the counselors. These are just a few examples of common limits.

While limits are a standard feature of many play therapy approaches, the exact type of limits used by a particular therapist really depends on the therapist's personality and the setting in which the therapy occurs. That is, some counselors simply cannot tolerate messes, so they might tend to place more limits on messy play. Toys being used might be more breakable, so there will be more limits around how the toys are used. Other counselors might have heavy duty unbreakable toys and, therefore, allow much rough-and-tumble play with the toys. The setting is also very important. At one point in my career, when I worked in a school setting, my office was right next to the main office with an entrance directly from that office. Occasionally, if a child became loud or rambunctious in play, the principal would stick his head in and give me a look that I called "the ray." So, until my office was soundproofed (which it eventually was) I had to be aware of the noise level and set some limits when a child became too loud.

Approaches to Limitsetting

There are two basic approaches to limitsetting. The first involves the use of a standard set of basic rules that serve as advanced organizers to the child. The second approach is situational, placing emphasis on allowing the child to discover limits through the setting of limits when limit testing behaviors occur. At least one of these approaches utilizes a standard procedure for limitsetting which will be described below.

Rules

The standard rules serve to orient the child to the play therapy situation and as referents when the child is engaging in an inappropriate behavior. Many play therapy approaches incorporate these types of standard rules into their procedures. An example of the rules I use is provided in Figure 3-1.

> 1. This is your special time. You may play with any of the toys in the room. You can play, talk, talk and play, or do nothing at all.
> 2. You are not allowed to hurt yourself or me.
> 3. You are not allowed to mess up yourself or me on purpose.
> 4. You are not allowed to break toys on purpose or take them out of the room.
> 5. Your time goes until ____ o'clock (or until the big hand is on the ____).
> 6. You don't have to clean up unless you want to.

FIGURE 3-1 BASIC PLAY THERAPY RULES

Limitsetting using this approach is fairly simple. When a child begins doing something that is against the rules, the therapist reminds the child about the rule. If the child persists in the limit testing behavior, the child is reminded one to two more times, after which, that particular play activity is stopped. After stopping the activity, it is important for the counselor to have the child move on with the play and not dwell on the particular limitsetting situation. Limitsetting is not intended to be punishment. It is a way of defining structure and boundaries for the child and helping the child internalize these boundaries.

EXAMPLE

A child who is finger painting begins to smear paint on the wall. The counselor says, "Jimmy, that is against the rules. Remember, one of the rules is that you can't mess up the room on purpose. Smearing paint on the wall is messing up the room. So you are not allowed to do that in here."

If the child persists in trying to paint the wall, the counselor says, "Jimmy, that's against the rules. If you keep trying to paint the wall, we will have to put the paint away for today." If the child continues to test the limits, the counselor matter-of-factly states,

"I guess you have chosen to put the paints away for today," and proceeds to put the paints away and wipe the child's hands. Then the counselor says, "What would you like to do now," and the play continues.

When using this approach, the rules should be general enough so that they can be used as referents for a variety of limit testing behaviors, and few enough in numbers to enable children to remember them clearly.

SITUATIONAL LIMITSETTING

Practitioners who use situational limitsetting believe that the use of rules interferes with the spontaneity of the child's play, stimulates limit testing that might not otherwise occur, and interferes with limit testing that might be necessary as part of the child's therapeutic process. Moreover, the goals of this type of limitsetting are slightly different in that this approach places more emphasis on the child's responsibility and decision making when a limitsetting situation arises.

Garry Landreth, in his Child-Centered play therapy approach (Landreth, 1991), provides a standard procedure for situational limitsetting which he calls the A-C-T model. When a limittesting behavior occurs, the counselor ACKNOWLEDGES the child's feeling or need, COMMUNICATES the limit, and TARGETS acceptable alternative behaviors. Landreth has also developed a unique kind of language for setting limits that utilizes the passive voice, eliminating an accusatory tone. Thus, in the example above, in which the child is painting the wall, rather than say, "You may not paint the wall," the counselor states, "The wall is not for painting," or "Finger paints are not for painting on the wall." This shift in voice is intended to circumvent a defensive response and open up the possibility for the child to consider the alternatives that are presented.

Landreth recommends that the child be given approximately "three strikes"–that is, three opportunities to stop the unacceptable behavior. Similar to the procedure above, if the child persists in the behavior, then a final choice is stated, which usually involves the consequence of giving up a particular toy or activity for the remainder of the session.

EXAMPLE

A child takes a rubber dart gun, places a dart in it, and points it at the counselor. The counselor states, "It looks like you want to shoot that dart at me (Acknowledges the child's desire), but I am not for shooting things at (Communicates limit). If you want to shoot at something, you can shoot at the target, the bobo doll, or other things that won't be hurt by the dart (Targets acceptable alternatives)."

If the child chooses to engage in one of the acceptable alternatives, then the play continues uninterrupted. However, if the child continues to engage in the limit testing behavior after three warnings, the counselor states the final choice, "If you continue to point the gun at me, we will have to put it away for the day. I am not for shooting things at." If the child continues at this point, the counselor, again matter-of-factly, puts the gun away and says, "It's clear that you have chosen not to play with the gun today. What would you like to do now?" The session then continues.

I have modified Landreth's approach in a couple of ways. Sometimes it is not possible to use the A-C-T procedure before the child has already done something that is damaging or potentially harmful. For instance, in the paint smearing example above, by the time I acknowledged the child's behavior, the wall would have already been painted. I call my modification the "I A-C-T" model, "I" standing for INTERRUPT the limit testing behavior. In the painting example, the first thing I would do is say the child's name firmly, call "time-out," or even gently hold the child's wrists to interrupt the action. Then, I would proceed to use the standard A-C-T model.

The second modification I have incorporated is to give the child more decision making in targeting alternative behaviors. Instead of my providing alternatives, I ask the child, "If you want to smear something with paint, what would be all right to use for smearing?" I then allow the child to formulate alternatives. It is my belief that if the child has input into the alternatives, he is more likely to choose one that is acceptable. In other words, it invests the child in the choice. If the child simply cannot think of alternative behaviors, then I offer some alternatives.

Combined Approach. The fact of the matter is that I often use a combination of the two limitsetting approaches described above. I have a set of standard rules, but when a limitsetting situation arises, I acknowledge the child's need, communicate the limit using the rules, and then ask the child to generate alternatives. In this way, I have been able to incorporate useful parts of both approaches into my limitsetting method.

EXAMPLE

A child begins to throw a rubber ball at a window in the playroom. The counselor holds the ball for a minute (Interupts the behavior), and says, "It looks like you want to bounce the ball off something (Acknowledges the child's desire). But remember, one of the rules is that you are not allowed to break something on purpose (Communicates the rule). If you throw a ball at the window, you might break the window. If you want to bounce the ball off something, what could you bounce it off of that wouldn't break or get hurt (Encourages child to target alternatives)?"

COMMON LIMITSETTING PITFALLS

Over the years, I have noticed some common problems that my students encounter with limitsetting as beginning play therapists. These include being overly tentative, lack of follow through, vagueness, sharing responsibility with the child, and being authoritarian. Novice play therapists display a strong tendency to be a little "wishy washy" when they set limits. This seems to be due to a number of possible factors, the primary one of which is fear of harming the therapeutic relationship. Other reasons for this include lack of confidence, discomfort with an authority role, and lack of experience with children.

Overtentativeness. The problem with being overly tentative is that the counselor fails to communicate to the child that the counselor means what she says. Thus, the child does not believe that he has to conform to the limit and simply ignores the counselor. The most typical situation in which I observe this is when a session is over and the counselor wants the child to leave the playroom. Beginning play therapists often will say very softly, "Time's up," almost asking the child's permission to leave. I usually allow them to repeat this three or four times before I give the counselor specific instructions via intercom to state this firmly to the child, take the child by the hand, turn off the lights, and leave. Once the counselor states clear limits and takes firm action, the child learns that the counselor means what he says.

Lack of follow through. The problem with inconsistent or no follow through when a limit is set is the same problem that parents experience when they fail to follow through on discipline. The child learns that nothing is going to happen, or that there is a chance that the child is going to get away with the inappropriate behavior. So, if a counselor sets a limit, either using rules or situational limitsetting, then she must back the limit up with consequences and action. If the counselor is unwilling to do this, then she shouldn't set the limit in the first place. Again, the child needs to learn that the counselor means what she says if the counselor and playroom are going to be predictable aspects of the child's life.

Vagueness. Beginning counselors sometimes have difficulty communicating limits to children clearly. In this case the counselor might state vaguely, "You shouldn't do that," or "That's against the rules," but not state exactly what the child should not be doing, or what rule is being violated. It is important to be specific about the limit and, if necessary, any consequences that might occur if the child persists in the inappropriate behavior.

Sharing responsibility. Sharing responsibility is simply the tendency to use what Landreth labels as "babysitter talk" (Landreth, 1991). This is the tendency to say, "We don't hit people in here," or "We don't throw sand." This seems to stem again from the counselor wanting to soften or sugar coat the message, as if the child or the relationship is too fragile to allow the adult to assume an appropriate role with the child. The counselor knows what she can and cannot do, so the message needs to be directed respectfully to the obvious recipient. Hence, counselors should state firmly to clients, "You are not allowed to..." or utilize Landreth's passive voice approach, "The sand is not for..." Place the responsibility where it belongs.

Being authoritarian. Taking an authoritarian stance is usually a product of not believing the child will listen to you. In these situations, the counselor takes over immediately and forces the child to conform without giving the child an opportunity to choose. If a goal of limitsetting is to foster personal responsibility and decision making skills, then authoritarianism is not going to facilitate this goal. Aside from situations in which the child is in physical danger, most limitsetting situations do not require the counselor to make the child do what the counselor wants her to do. Thus, it is important to use the language of choice and to allow the child a reasonable, albeit not infinite, amount of time to make a decision regarding the limit. For example, instead of stating, "You're done with the sandbox," when the child throws sand, say, "If you choose to throw sand, you are choosing to not use the sandbox today." That small shift in language makes an immense difference in the message.

LIMITSETTING PRACTICE

It is time to practice some basic limitsetting response skills. For each of the following vignettes, first decide if this would be a limitsetting situation for YOU. Then, assume that you have to set a limit, cover the suggested responses, and formulate one response based on the rules approach, a second based on the I A-C-T model, and a third combined response. Then, compare your responses to the suggested responses that are provided. Remember, there is a range of appropriate responses. The suggested responses simply provide some ideas of possible responses that might be used in each situation. After completing this exercise, continue your practice through the simulation activity at the end of the chapter.

Practice Vignettes

Directions: Read each vignette and decide how you might respond if you were working with the child. Sample responses are provided.

1. **Child begins throwing blocks at you.**
   Limitsetting situation for you?   ❑ Yes   ❑ No

Rule Response:
Remember, it's against the rules to hurt me on purpose, and throwing blocks at me might hurt me.

I A-C-T Response:
(Stopping the child from throwing first) Looks like you want to throw blocks at me, but blocks are not for throwing at people. If you want to throw the blocks at something that won't get hurt or break, what can you throw the blocks at? [OR: If you want to throw blocks, you may throw them at the bobo doll or the stuffed animals.]
OR
Looks like you want to throw blocks at me, but I am not for throwing things at. If you want to throw blocks at something, what can you use that won't get broken?
OR
Looks like you want to throw blocks at me, but I am not for throwing blocks at. If you want to throw something at me, you may use the nerf ball or a stuffed animal.

Combined Approach:
Looks like you want to throw blocks at me, but it's against the rules to hurt me, and blocks would hurt me if I get hit. If you want to throw something at me, what could you throw that won't hurt me? [OR: If you want to throw blocks, what could you throw them at that wouldn't hurt or break something?]

2. **Child stops in the middle of playing, goes to the door and opens it to leave the room.**
   Limitsetting situation for you?   ❑ Yes   ❑ No

Rule Approach: _____

_____

_____

I A-C-T Approach: _____

_____

_____

Combined Approach: _____

_____

_____

Chapter Three: Limitsetting

Suggested Responses:
  Rule Approach: (Go to the door and hold it gently to stop the child from leaving.) This is your special time and the rule is that you have to stay here until the big hand is on the six (or until 9:30, etc.). I'm wondering why you want to leave right now.
  I A-C-T: (Go to the door and hold it gently to stop the child from leaving.) Looks like you want to leave right now, but it's not time for leaving. If you want to be away from me, what could you do in the room to be away from me?
  Combined: (Go to the door and hold it gently to stop the child from leaving.) This is your special time and the rule is that you have to stay here until the big hand is on the six (or until 9:30, etc.). I'm wondering why you want to leave right now. If you want to be away from me, what could you do in the room to be away from me?

3. **While smearing finger paints heavily on paper, the child stops, turns to you with his hands, and moves forward to smear you.**
  Limitsetting situation for you?   ❏ Yes   ❏ No

Rule Approach: _____

_____

_____

I A-C-T Approach: _____

_____

_____

Combined Approach: _____

_____

_____

Suggested Responses:
  Rule Approach: (Stop the child by gently holding his wrists while you speak.) Looks like you really want to smear me. But that would mess me up and messing me up is against the rules.
  I A-C-T: (Interrupt the child by gently holding his wrists while you speak.) Looks like you really want to smear me. Finger paints are not for smearing on people. If you want to smear the finger paints, what do you think would be okay to smear them on? [OR: ...you may smear them on the paper, the easel, or the table.]
  Combined: (Stop the child by gently holding his wrists while you speak.) Looks like you really want to smear me. But that would mess me up and messing me up is against the rules. If you want to smear the finger paints, what do you think would be okay to smear them on? [OR: ...you may smear them on the paper, the easel, or the table.]

4. **Child is banging on the play house with a hammer and finally tips the house over.**
   Limitsetting situation for you? ❏ Yes ❏ No

   Rule Approach:_____
   _____
   _____

   I A-C-T Approach: _____
   _____
   _____

   Combined Approach: _____
   _____
   _____

   Suggested Approaches
   Rule Approach: Looks like you are really mad and want to hit that house. But hitting the house with the hammer might break it, and one of the rules is that you are not allowed to break things in here.
   I A-C-T: You are really mad and want to hit that. But the house is not for hitting with the hammer. If you want to hit something with the hammer, you can hit the workbench or the table.
   Combined: Looks like you are really mad and want to hit that house. But hitting the house with the hammer might break it, and one of the rules is that you are not allowed to break things in here. If you want to hit something with the hammer to show you are mad, what can you hit that won't get broken? [OR: If you want to hit the house, what can you use that won't damage it?]

5. **Child goes to roll all the Play-Doh in the sandbox.**
   Limitsetting situation for you? ❏ Yes ❏ No

   Rule Approach:_____
   _____
   _____

   I A-C-T Approach: _____
   _____
   _____

Chapter Three: Limitsetting

Combined Approach: _____
_____
_____

Suggested Responses:
   Rule Approach: You want to put the Play-Doh in the sandbox, but that's against the rules because that would wreck the Play-Doh.
   I A-C-T: (Interrupt the child by saying her name firmly or blocking the sandbox gently with your hand.) You want to put the Play-Doh in the sandbox, but the Play-Doh is not for putting in the sand. What are other things that you could do with the Play-Doh? [OR: ...with the sand?]
   Combined: You want to put the Play-Doh in the sandbox, but that's against the rules because that would wreck the Play-Doh. What are other things that you could do with the Play-Doh? [OR: ...with the sand?]

Directions: Now, use the approach indicated for each vignette. Again, cover the suggested response and compare your response after you are finished.

6. **Child begins sprinkling and gently tossing sand onto the table and floor.**
   Limitsetting situation for you?   ❏ Yes   ❏ No

Rule Approach: _____
_____
_____

Suggested Response: Spilling sand like that is against the rules because that is messing things up on purpose. Sand stays in the sandbox.

7. **Child begins playing with the window shade, pulling on it hard enough to pull it off the window.**
   Limitsetting situation for you?   ❏ Yes   ❏ No

I A-C-T Approach: _____
_____
_____

Suggested Response: You really want to make that go up and down, but the shade is not for playing with. So, you may decide if you want it up or down, and then you may choose to play with the toys in the room.

8. Child gets upset and kicks you in the shin.
    Limitsetting situation for you?　　❏ Yes　❏ No

Combined Approach: _____

_____

_____

Suggested Response: You are very angry, but kicking me is against the rules, because you are not allowed to hurt me. If you want to kick something, what can you kick that won't hurt me or you, or break anything?

9. Child points a toy gun at you after you set a limit for another behavior.
    Limitsetting situation for you?　　❏ Yes　❏ No

I A-C-T Approach: _____

_____

_____

Suggested Response: It looks like you are upset and want to show me by pretending to shoot me. But guns are not for pointing at people in here. If you want to pretend to shoot someone, what can you use as a pretend person? [OR: What are other ways you can show me you are upset with me?]

10. Child begins to throw Play-Doh balls around the room.
    Limitsetting situation for you?　　❏ Yes　❏ No

Combined Approach: _____

_____

_____

Suggested Response: Remember, one of the rules is that you are not allowed to wreck toys or damage the room on purpose. Throwing Play-Doh balls messes the room up on purpose and wrecks the Play Doh. If you want to throw something, what can you use that won't break these rules? [OR: If you want to throw Play-Doh, how and where can you do it so it won't break the rules?]

Special Limitsetting Situations

There are two particular limitsetting situations which I have found require some specialized approaches to setting limits. The first of these involves children who are hyperactive or overstimulated in the playroom. These children tend to move through the playroom like tornadoes, randomly picking up toys and playing momentarily, then moving on to other toys. They spend only a few minutes focusing on any particular toy and lose interest quickly. This type of play is different from the exploratory play of initial sessions in that, in exploratory play, children usually spend more time trying out toys, and eventually focus on one or two play activities. The type of play I am describing here is random, rapid, and unfocused. It is a repeated pattern that occurs over two or more sessions.

With these type of overstimulated clients, I use a more structured type of therapy during the initial stages of counseling. First, I establish a baseline of the approximate length of time that the child can maintain focus with any particular toy by timing the child during the unfocused play. Then, I establish the following rule:

"When you come in the room, you may *choose* one toy to play with. You must continue to play with that toy until the big hand on the clock is on____(I indicate the baseline time to the child). You may not switch to another toy until I tell you it is time to do so. When the big hand reaches____I will let you know. Then you can *choose* another toy or *choose* to continue playing with the toy that you have. Do you understand?"

I then implement the procedure, gradually increasing the time intervals over several sessions (usually two to three). When the child can maintain focus on one play activity for a reasonable amount of time (10 minutes, for instance), then I shift to the regular playroom rules. If the child backslides into the same type of unfocused play, I repeat the procedure.

The second type of special limitsetting situation is a perseverative type of play in which children are unable to discontinue particular play activities. Children do this for a number of reasons. Children with certain types of brain disorders, such as autism, Asperger's syndrome, and obsessive-compulsive disorder will engage in this type of play almost as if they are broken records stuck in a groove. Highly anxious children will also stay with "safe" and familiar situations because of their uncertainty about the playroom structure. In these situations I use a reverse of the previous procedure. These children MUST change activities after a certain period of time. Thus, I give them the following directions: "When I tell you it's time, you have to choose another toy to play with." If the child does not respond when told, then I sometimes have to take the child by the hand, move her away from the toy and direct her to choose another toy.

The Truth About Limitsetting

A few years back, I set out to do some observational research on limitsetting. I collected dozens of hours of videotapes of actual play therapy sessions that occurred at the Alfred University Child and Family Services Center over the course of one year. At the end of the year, I asked two of my graduate assistants to do some trial observations of limitsetting techniques. They were unable to do this for one very important reason. Limit testing situations simply did not occur frequently enough to provide an adequate number of observations for the research. In fact, the modal (or most frequently occurring) number of limitsetting situations per session was zero, and the mean, less than one. So, after spending a whole chapter reading about and practicing limitsetting, you now know the truth–it simply does not occur all that often.

There are certain points during the therapeutic process at which more limit testing occurs. But even then, it usually consists of no more than two or three incidents in one session. There are also certain types of kids who tend to test limits more, particularly angry, defiant children. However, the reality is that beginning play therapists tend to worry more about the potential for limit testing than they need to. It's not that big a deal!

The second truth about limitsetting is that there is little or no research about what limitsetting approaches are effective, and whether one approach is more effective than another. Most of the existing ideas about limitsetting that have been presented here and elsewhere are based on clinical experiences and philosophies of a few experts in the field. Thus, if you are more child-centered, you might subscribe to an approach that is closer to Landreth's A-C-T model. If you are more behaviorally oriented, you might use reinforcement contingencies. These ideas are based upon certain viewpoints about how children should be treated in therapy. Further research is needed to help us understand what really works, or what may actually be damaging in these situations. Time will tell.

HOMEWORK ASSIGNMENT

LIMITSETTING SIMULATIONS

You should now continue on with your simulation practice, but this time focus on practicing limitsetting responses. You will again need an adult partner to serve as a "child." Choose the child role from the list of vignettes below. Then spend two 30 minute sessions responding to your client's play, and in particular, to the limit testing behaviors that your client presents to you. Complete the self-assessment form at the end of this chapter in order to review your reaction to these practice sessions.

LIMITSETTING ROLES

Client 1:
Four-year-old who likes to make messes.

Client 2:
Limit testing six-year-old.

Client 3:
Angry seven-year-old who needs to discharge anger.

Client 4:
Eight year-old who wants to do the opposite of anything adults tell him (her) to do.

Client 5:
Ten-year-old whose parents were recently separated. Play focuses on controlling the counselor.

Client 6:
Eleven-year-old low achiever who needs to have the upper hand with adults.

Play Session Self Assessment

1. With which toys did you feel most comfortable? Why?

2. With which toys did you feel most uncomfortable? Why?

3. Did you experience any particular thoughts in relation to certain play activities (memories, visualizations, etc.)?

   Play Activity   Thought

4. Did you experience any strong feelings in relation to certain play activities?

   Play Activity   Feeling

5. What limitsetting situations occurred, and how did you respond to them?

6. List any questions you have about play therapy at this point.
   Limitsetting Situation   Response

7. Rate your comfort level with play therapy.

        1   2   3   4   5   6   7

   Very Uncomfortable   Very Comfortable

Continue on to the next chapter.

Chapter 4

Multicultural Issues in Play Therapy

Cultural Attitudes Pretest

Directions: Before reading this chapter, honestly respond to the statements at right using the following scale.

1 = Strongly Disagree
2 = Disagree
3 = Agree
4 = Strongly Agree

Some of these statements reflect attitudes, while others reflect facts. Review the statements and identify statements where your response might be based on misinformation. Then, go to data sources that might provide such information (government agency, professional organization, and university data bases on the Internet, books, or other resources available in libraries.) After doing this and reading this chapter, decide which responses you might change.

___ 1. Multiculturalism deals primarily with race issues.
___ 2. Basic counseling skills are applicable across cultural groups.
___ 3. Most welfare recipients would prefer staying on welfare because it is convenient.
___ 4. I feel very comfortable around gay males.
___ 5. All blacks in the US prefer to be identified as African-Americans.
___ 6. Asian-American students tend to be higher achievers because their families are more concerned about achievement than are families of other minority group students.
___ 7. Lesbians are typically more masculine in appearance.
___ 8. Cultural differences are related more to racial differences between counselor and client.
___ 9. White counselors can never really understand minority clients' problems.
___ 10. Minority counselors can never really understand white clients' problems.
___ 11. I feel comfortable among a group of individuals that is different from the people with whom I typically have contact.
___ 12. I am concerned about AIDS when I am around gay men.
___ 13. Formal counseling is always the best option when individuals are experiencing emotional problems.
___ 14. If a counselor is skilled at establishing solid relationships with clients, culture becomes a non-issue.
___ 15. Individuals who are more fully assimilated into the majority culture are better candidates for counseling.
___ 16. Juvenile crime is primarily an inner city phenomenon.
___ 17. Differences between cultural groups have a greater impact on counseling than differences within cultural groups.
___ 18. If I had my choice, I would provide services only to people of my racial group.
___ 19. All people are basically the same.
___ 20. Socio-economic status tends to be less important when looking at differences between cultural groups.

INTRODUCTION

Over the past two decades, the mental health fields have become more concerned about the impact of cultural differences on the provision of counseling and mental health services (Lee, 1995). Research in the 1960's and 70's suggested that clients hailing from cultural backgrounds that were different from the mainstream, Eurocentric, majority culture of the United States (white, male, and middle class) may: 1) view psychotherapy and counseling differently; 2) have communication styles that are inconsistent with styles that are expected in traditional forms of therapy; and 3) have values and world views that differ substantially from the logic-based, scientific views of psychology and psychiatry (Herring, 1997). For a long period of time, the psychotherapy fields adopted a deficit view of culturally different individuals. Clients from these groups were seen as being inferior to typical middle class white clients, thus, needing to adapt their world views and styles to fit the therapy. This resulted in such phenomena as inflated diagnosis rates of serious psychopathology among African-American clients (Korchin, 1980) and high rates of drop-outs among minority group clients (Sue, 1977).

Since the late 1970's there has been a shift away from this deficit viewpoint to one which values cultural differences and seeks to adapt traditional psychotherapy and counseling approaches to be useful within the various world views of clients from different cultural groups. Fueled by the seminal work of Sue (1977), Sue and Sue (1977), Lazare, Eisenthal, and Wasserman (1975), and Pedersen (1984), multicultural counseling has assumed the role of a basic assumption that undergirds most counseling approaches today. This chapter is intended to serve as a brief introduction to multicultural issues in counseling in general, and play therapy in particular. General suggestions will be made on how to pay attention to cultural differences within the context of the basic play therapy skills discussed in previous chapters. Information regarding counseling issues of specific cultural groups is available in texts by Lee (1995), Pedersen (1988), Sue and Sue (1990), and others.

WHAT IS CULTURE?

Before cultural differences can be discussed, we must have a common frame of reference regarding what constitutes "culture." When we talk about multiculturalism or cultural differences, most people think about racial or ethnic differences. While race and ethnicity were original focuses of the multicultural field, the scope of what we call culture has expanded considerably. Pedersen (1991) defines culture very broadly as including "demographic variables (e.g., age, sex, place of residence), status variables (e.g., social, educational, economic, and affiliations (formal and informal), as well as ethnographic variables such as nationality, ethnicity, language, and religion" (Pedersen, p. 7). Within this framework, culture expands to include such areas as socioeconomic status (e.g., the "culture of poverty"), sexual preference (e.g., gay vs. straight culture), and even region of the country from which one hails (e.g., Southern culture). I once had a student who relocated from New York City to an apartment on the edge of the very rural town in which Alfred University is located. Being accustomed to the high density of housing in the city, her perception was that she had moved to a wilderness area, and she was, thus, convinced that she needed to purchase a gun to protect herself from wild animals. When she discussed this with me, I informed her that, by Alfred standards, she was residing in a town in which the houses just happened to be several hundred feet apart. According to the broad definition of culture, these differences in perceptions are related to differences between urban and rural cultures. In other words, one person's wilderness is another's neighborhood.

What definition of culture is most useful within the practice of play therapy? Certainly ethnic and racial differences are the most obvious in terms of impacting both what children play with and how children play. Socioeconomic status is also an important factor, there being convincing evidence that children from lower SES groups tend to be less verbal than those from middle and upper SES groups (Berger, 1991). Other factors that need to be considered are such things as religious orientation and sex differences. For instance, children who hail from very conservative religious groups may have been taught that it is disrespectful to interact with adults as equals, or that psychotherapy is evil. (I have experienced these views first hand many times in my career.)

What is important to keep in mind when counseling children is that children, even more than adults, are products of their cultures. This has to do with the fact that children function within a context in which they have no control over the adults in their environments, and these adults teach and model the values and beliefs that become children's cultures. Until adolescence, family is the primary influence on children, and because children want to please the significant adults in their lives, they are unlikely to question the beliefs that they are being taught. Therefore, culture is probably an even more powerful influence over children than it is with adult clients. Play therapists, then, must pay attention to this influence and modify their approaches to be consistent with cultural factors that may impact the counseling process.

THE BETWEEN VERSUS WITHIN GROUP DIFFERENCES DILEMMA

When we talk about cultural differences, we are focusing on the *differences* between cultural groups. This can encompass such aspects of culture as physical attributes, dress, food, holidays, and traditions, as well as beliefs and values. However, these differences are generalizations about members of a particular culture as a *group* and do not apply to all *individuals* in that cultural group. This is the crux of the "between" versus "within" group differences debate in the multicultural counseling field. Between group differences are the general differences that exist among cultural groups. Within group differences are the ways in which individuals within a group differ from the general characteristics or beliefs of that group. For instance, even within what we call majority culture in the US, there are regional differences reflected in dialects, foods, and local customs.

A dilemma occurs for a counselor when he/she is confronted with a client who belongs to a particular non-majority cultural group. If the counselor assumes, based on appearance or other information, that the individual conforms to the general characteristics of that cultural group, without any knowledge of the client as an individual, the counselor is, in effect, stereotyping. In elementary statistics, we learn that the distribution of traits in nature forms the normal or bell curve. Within such a distribution, more than one-fourth of individuals in a particular group deviate from the norms of that group to some extent, with about five percent doing so substantially (Gay, 1976). Thus, many individuals who hail from specific cultural groups may not fit the general characteristics or belief systems connected with those groups.

Counselors, then, have the responsibility of striking a balance between acknowledging cultural differences, while at the same time recognizing how clients differ from their cultural groups. This requires that counselors develop working knowledge of world views, communication styles, and customs of various cultures with which they will come into contact. At the same time, counselors must be careful not to use this knowledge to stereotype individuals, rather to understand clients within the context of their individual cultural experiences.

How does one do this? Certainly learning *about* cultures in standard ways (reading, classes) is helpful. But nothing substitutes for experiencing different cultures, or hearing about and discussing cultural differences with members of different cultures. And when working with clients who are culturally different from me, I ask them about things that I don't know or don't understand related to their cultures. A few years ago, I worked with a child whose family was part of the Mennonite sect. While I knew a little general information about Mennonites, having had some contact with members of this sect while living in another area of the country, I realized that I needed to know a lot more in order to work with this child. So, I confessed my ignorance to the child's parents, and asked for their guidance regarding whether or not something that was occurring in therapy was inconsistent with their belief system. This proved to be a wonderful learning experience about cultural differences related to religion.

It is also helpful to examine your own cultural identity and think about how that influences your belief system and perceptions. The activity shown below and on the following page is designed to help you start doing this.

WHO AM I?

1. If you are a U.S. citizen, how do you identify your ethnic group?

_____White   If you identify yourself as a member of a specific national group,
                        please state your affiliation:_____.

_____Black   If you identify yourself as a member of a specific national group,
_____African-American   please state your affiliation:_____.

_____Hispanic   If you identify yourself as a member of a specific national group,
_____Latino   please state your affiliation:_____.

_____Asian   If you identify yourself as a member of a specific national group,
_____Asian-American   please state your affiliation:_____.
_____Amerasian

_____Native American   If you identify yourself as a member of a specific tribal nation,
                        please state your affiliation:_____.
_____American

2. If you are not a U.S. citizen, how do you identify your ethnic group?
   _____

3. How many generations of your family, before your generation, were born in the US? _____

4. Rank the following in level of importance regarding your cultural identity
   (1 = Most Important, 5 = Least Important):
   _____National Origin
   _____Race
   _____Gender
   _____Sexual Orientation
   _____Religion
   _____US Region of Origin
   _____Region of Other Country of Origin

5. Respond to the statements below using the following ratings:
   1 = Not Important 2=Somewhat Important 3=Important 4=Very Important

   _____Eating foods specific to your cultural group.

   _____Observing traditions specific to your cultural group.

   _____Attending cultural gatherings specific to your cultural group.

   _____Spending a significant amount of non-work, non-school time with members of your cultural group.

   _____Avoiding non-work, non-school related contact with members of other cultural groups.

   _____Speaking the language of your culture.

   _____Avoiding non-work, non-school related contact with members of the majority culture.

   _____Marrying an individual within your cultural group.

   _____Passing on traditions, language, etc. of your cultural group to your children.

Indicate on the following continuum where you see yourself in relation to your culture and the majority culture.

|—————|—————|—————|—————|

Strong identity with your own cultural group/ Weak identity with majority culture.

Identify about equally with your own cultural group and the majority culture.

Strong identity with the majority culture/Weak identity with own cultural group.

Multicultural Considerations in Play Therapy

The skills and guidelines discussed in previous chapters are based on traditional ideas about play therapy which are decidedly Eurocentric. Play therapy as we think about it today is rooted in traditional psychotherapeutic ideas espoused by mostly white males and a few white females. Since World War II, there has also been a strong influence of mainstream culture in the United States. While there is some history of using play therapy in this country with non-majority populations, particularly African-American children, not much has been written about or researched regarding the use of play therapy with non-Western, non majority clients. This does not mean that play therapy is not useful with these types of clients, since play, again, is universal. It simply means that if you are working with non-majority clients you need to pay attention to cultural differences that may influence the therapeutic situation. Some suggestions are provided below that may help beginning play therapists pay attention to cultural differences.

Age Ranges. Cultural differences may impact the applicable age ranges for play therapy. In many non-Western cultures, individuals are considered to be adults at considerably lower ages, such as 13 or 14, than they are in European-oriented cultures. Thus, forcing a 10- or 11-year old child into a play therapy situation may actually be insulting and aversive. In this case it is important to understand the cultural background of the children with whom you are working and to only provide play therapy to individuals who a particular culture, based on age, identifies as children.

Toy Selection. A second issue is the choice of toys used in the playroom. While most cultural groups in the US have some exposure to the toys suggested in Chapter 1, some regional differences do exist. A simple but obvious difference here is the types of animal figures provided in the playroom. Farm animals are much more common for rural children, but not necessarily part of the experiences of urban children. Domestic and zoo animals are the types with which urban children may be more familiar. A more pronounced difference might be evident with children who are recent immigrants from less developed European countries and non-European countries. Differences in toys for children from these groups may include types of dolls and puppets, style of dollhouse, and even the type of art media that they use. If working with clients from these groups, counselors should find out from their clients what types of toys are familiar to them, and then try to adapt the toys in the playroom or provide alternative toys that match the clients' cultural backgrounds.

Counselors who work in situations in which they are providing services to a completely non-Western population may elect to use few, if any, of the traditional play therapy toys. In this case, the toys that are included in the playroom will be those that are common to the culture, which also are therapeutically useful as determined by guidelines discussed in Chapter 1. By doing this, counselors acknowledge clients' cultural experiences, utilize the resources specific to the culture, and avoid the trap of trying to fit the client to the therapy.

Playroom Structure. Children from certain cultural groups may have some difficulties with playrooms that are inconsistent with their cultural groups' norms for orderliness or organization. That is, for some cultural groups, a high degree of structure and orderliness might be the norm, while for others, a more casual, less structured environment is typical. Play therapists need to be prepared to adjust the structure and organization of their playrooms if this appears to interfere with the therapy of culturally different clients.

Response and Attending Skills. The SKILLED framework for attending skills discussed in Chapter 2 is an area that may be significantly affected by cultural differences. Different cultures have different norms for such things as adult-child interactions and physical proximity and distance in social situations. For instance, if a child is from a culture in which respect for adults is highly valued, the child may be less likely to initiate play activities, relying on the adult for direction and permission. For the child to do otherwise would be disrespectful. In this situation, the play therapist may have to conform to the child's cultural norms, recognize that the child needs to receive permission from the therapist, and initiate play activities.

Cultures develop conventions governing interpersonal space in social situations. Take, for example, the experience of standing in a packed elevator in our culture. As soon as people enter an elevator, conversation stops, eye contact is avoided, and most people stare at the floor indicator. This is a convention that has evolved in our culture. This same type of norm exists for the types of interpersonal interactions that occur in the playroom. In some cultures, it may be an intrusion or sign of disrespect for a child to sit close to or on the same level as an adult. In other cultures, face-to-face interactions are uncomfortable. In these types of situations, counselors need to adapt the SKILLED framework and position themselves in relation to the client in a way that is culturally congruent and, therefore, comfortable for the client.

The manner in which a counselor responds therapeutically to the client may also be influenced by cultural differences. The types of attending responses described in Chapter 2 may be relatively intrusive and uncomfortable for individuals whose cultural norms for communication rely more on non-verbal communication, or who are members of cultures that value silence. The counselor's adaptation to such cultural norms should be, at minimum, a reduction in the frequency of responses. However, counselors may also have to modify their responding behavior more radically by eliminating verbal responses and relying on such non-verbal behaviors as *mirroring*. Mirroring is simply engaging in a behavior that is similar to the client's, in this case a similar type of play. It is a way of demonstrating to the client that you are attending to what she/he is doing. Concomitantly, this type of response acknowledges the client's cultural norm.

The issue in these examples is recognizing and respecting the norms of clients' cultural experiences. Gunnison (1999) has discussed the importance of *matching* the client as a means of being consistent with the client's experience. Matching can encompass such things as emulating the client's posture, conversation volume, and seating position. With culturally different clients, matching also includes attending to clients' needs for personal space, minimal eye contact, asking permission, and silence. This is all part of synchronizing oneself with clients' cultural norms, and, hence, their experiences. Through matching, counselors can attend to both between group and within group differences; that is, general cultural differences and unique characteristics of the individual.

Limitsetting. Concerns related to limitsetting are similar to those of responding. The primary issues are the communication and discipline styles of a particular culture. These areas are important in helping play therapists determine how children of different cultures recognize that limits are being set. For instance, if the discipline style within a specific culture is more physical and action oriented, then verbal limits might not be recognized by children of this culture. An approach like the A-C-T model would not necessarily be appropriate in this case. The play therapist might have to be more immediately active in setting limits, such as gently holding a child's hands to stop an unacceptable behavior. When dealing with children from cultures where it is the norm for parents to set limits through directives, the play therapist might have to simply tell the child what not to do, rather than give choices. As with responding, the goal is to match the child's cultural experience, and not to force the child to conform to the Eurocentric therapeutic norms.

Summary

The information that has been provided in this chapter is necessarily vague. As is true of other issues related to play therapy, little research exists on the impact of culture on play therapy. Only a few studies have appeared in professional publications that involve the use of play therapy with ethnic and racial minorities (Chau & Landreth, 1997; Trostle, 1988). Thus, we are again forced to look to clinical experience and research with adults and adolescents as guides in this area. The literature does provide information regarding general norms for specific cultural groups (Sue & Sue, 1990), and multicultural issues in the counseling and psychotherapy field. But it will be some time before solid research-based information on multicultural issues in play therapy exists.

Homework

It is time to re-examine your attitudes regarding individuals who are culturally different from you. Whether you are a member of the majority culture or of a minority cultural group, you most likely have some blindspots--attitudes, uncomfortable feelings, unresolved issues--regarding certain cultural groups that may interfere with your effectiveness as a helper. Because within-group differences also influence the counseling process, you may also have blindspots concerning individuals from your own cultural group.

Go back and review your responses on the previous activities in this chapter, then complete the items on the next two pages. Remember, the purpose of this module is to help you become aware of your own cross-cultural issues. Be thoughtful and honest in completing this activity. You might not have blindspots in all the areas listed--don't feel compelled to have a blindspot if one does not exist. Just be honest with yourself.

Cultural Blindspots

Racial Blindspots:

Ethnic Blindspots:

Religious Blindspots:

Gender Blindspots:

Sexual Orientation Blindspots:

Other Cultural Blindspots:

REMEDIATION PLAN

Directions: Now select the one or two blindspots that you see as most detrimental to your performance as a counselor and think about how you might overcome them.

Blindspot #1
Goal: _____

Activities for Overcoming Blindspot:

1. _____
   _____

2. _____
   _____

3. _____
   _____

Blindspot #2
Goal: _____

Activities for Overcoming Blindspot:

1. _____
   _____

2. _____
   _____

3. _____
   _____

Chapter 5

The First Session

In the previous four chapters, you reviewed the basic microskills in play therapy and should have practiced these skills to some extent in your simulation sessions. Now it is time to examine how to initiate the counseling process with a child. This chapter will present some practical procedures for beginning counseling with a child, that is, starting the first session.

The "first session" really encompasses portions of two sessions, an orientation session followed by the actual first play therapy session. The orientation session is a pre-therapy, "getting to know you" session that, with the exception of crisis situations, should occur prior to the first play therapy session. In this session, I meet with the child individually to help the child understand what happens in counseling, obtain some general information about the child from his or her perspective, and give the child an opportunity to get to know me. The content and sequence of this session usually includes: 1) explaining why the client has been referred for counseling; 2) orienting the client to the counseling situation; 3) discussing the client's likes and dislikes; 4) having the client complete family drawings and/or a genogram (family tree); and 5) allowing the client to ask questions they may have about the counselor or counseling situation. Each of these areas will be reviewed below.

In mental health settings and in school settings, when possible, I also spend time doing this same type of activity with the client's parents. In school settings, the individual orientation should also be supplemented by general group orientations with children, parents, and school staff. Chapter 11 provides information and materials for conducting such activities with the latter two groups. Group orientations with children will be discussed later in this chapter.

Explaining the Reason for Referral

One common question trainees pose to me is whether or not to tell a child why they are being seen by a counselor. Some experts in the field of play therapy are absolutely opposed to this, feeling that such information influences the client's play in one of the following ways. Child-centered therapists feel that telling children why they are in therapy organizes their play around presenting issues, thus interfering with their freedom to direct the therapy (Landreth, 1991). Practitioners of more general approaches, such as Developmental Play Therapy (Brody, 1997) see no utility in providing this information, as their approaches are designed to address broader, underlying issues, rather than specific presenting problems. These objections are based on philosophical positions rather than concrete evidence that explaining to children why they are in therapy has any negative impact on the therapeutic situation.

I disagree with the above positions, and my perspective is rooted in the PEGS. If I am to show *respect* for a client and be *genuine*, then it is my responsibility to explain to the client why he or she is in counseling. An adult client would *expect* an honest explanation. A child client is owed this, particularly because children usually have no input into the decision to enter counseling. Since adults make this decision, adults at least should provide children with an explanation for the decision. It is a simple case of respect.

How the decision to enter counseling is explained to a child is a different matter, and is based on the child's level of cognitive development and functioning, and the type of problem. Explanations should be developmentally appropriate, simple, and brief. If children want more information or a more complicated explanation, they usually ask. If this happens, then the counselor can provide additional information until clients indicate they are satisfied.

EXAMPLE 1: Classroom Behavior Problem

Counselor: Ben, your teacher asked me to see you because she thinks you are having trouble getting along with other kids in class. Do you know what she's talking about?

Client: *No.*

Counselor: Well, she said you have been in a couple of fights this past week because you didn't like what other kids said to you.

Client: *Oh yeah, but they started it.*

Counselor: So it seems to you that they started it. That's what we are going to try and work on here. Etc.

EXAMPLE 2: Sexual Abuse

Counselor: Katie, do you know why you are here today?

Client: *No.*

Counselor: Your mother and the caseworker are concerned about how you are feeling. They think you are feeling bad right now. Do you know what they are talking about?

Client: *I don't know.*

Counselor: They are worried about how you feel about being touched on your private parts by_____.

Client: *I don't want to talk about that.*

Counselor: You don't have to talk about that right now. I just want you to know why your mom wanted you to see me.

ORIENTATION TO THE COUNSELING SITUATION

WHY ORIENT CLIENTS?

Entering counseling or therapy is usually a new experience for most clients which can produce a considerable amount of anxiety and confusion regarding the situation itself. This is related to the fact that most people have little or no idea about what happens in counseling. Most of their preconceptions come from media portrayals of psychotherapy which, at minimum, are inaccurate. It behooves therapists, then, to provide clients with enough information about the counseling process to correct misperceptions and help reduce anxiety about the counseling situation.

A body of research has accumulated over the past 40 years which suggests that both adults and children benefit from pre-counseling orientation activities. Research with adults has demonstrated that pre-counseling orientation procedures are effective in helping clients develop expectations of psychotherapy that are congruent with those of therapists (Doster, 1975; Strupp & Bloxom, 1973). Clients who participated in orientation activities also rated their level of improvement higher than those who did not (Hoyt, 1979; Strupp & Bloxom; Zwick & Attkisson, 1985). Research with children suggests that use of pre-counseling orientation procedures helps to lower drop-out and missed appointment rates, and results in clients developing more realistic expectations of counseling, and improved client preferences for their therapists (Bonner & Everett, 1986; Day & Reznikoff, 1980; Francois, 1977; Holmes & Urie, 1975). A number of orientation approaches have been effective, including individual interviews, group presentations, audiotape presentations, and video presentations (Bonner & Everett; Cerio, 1993; Day & Reznikoff; Doster; Francois; Frank et al., 1959; Holmes & Urie; Hoyt; Park & Williams, 1986; Strupp & Bloxom; Zarchan, 1977; Zwick & Attkisson).

What does this mean to you as a play therapist? It would seem that providing some type of orientation to children and their parents would facilitate the therapeutic process by helping clients develop expectations of therapy that are consistent with what actually happens in therapy. Orientation really breaks down into two main areas: *cognitive* orientation involves conveying information about what happens in therapy; *affective* orientation involves conveying a sense of who the therapist is as a person. The former can be accomplished by supplying information, while the latter requires more time and contact with the therapist.

COGNITIVE ORIENTATION.
Information provided in the cognitive orientation includes the following.

1. A general definition of what a counselor and what counseling or therapy are.
2. Specific information about the counselor's therapeutic approach, in this case, play therapy.
3. Information about the behavior or techniques the client may observe the counselor using.
4. Information about what the client is expected to do in therapy.
5. The frequency of sessions.
6. The typical length of treatment.
7. Confidentiality and its limits.
8. Involvement of others in the therapy (teachers, parents, relatives, etc.).

EXAMPLE: Individual Play Therapy Orientation

General Introduction to Counseling: I am a counselor, and a counselor sees kids who are feeling bad or having trouble with their behavior or having trouble getting along with other kids. Do you have trouble with anything like this? (Wait for the client's response.)
What counselors do is listen to kids, or watch them play, or help them figure out ways to feel better or solve their problems.
Specific Information About Counselor's Approach: You have probably looked around my room and seen a lot of toys. When you come here, I will be watching you play with those toys.
Information About What the Client is Expected to Do: You can play, talk, talk and play or do nothing at all. It's up to you.
Information About the Counselor's Behaviors: And what I will be doing is watching and trying to understand what you are doing, how you are feeling, and sharing this with you. (The counselor will also state the rules at this time, if the counselor is using the rule-oriented approach to limitsetting.)
Frequency and Length of Sessions: You will be seeing me every week on Tuesday, and your time will be from when the big hand is on the 12 to when the big hand is on the six. I will let you know when your time is almost over, and when I say time is up, that means you have to stop what you are doing and leave with me.
Length of Treatment: I can't tell you yet just how long you will be seeing me. But I can say that most kids who have problems like yours see me more than five or six times before things start to get better for them.
Confidentiality: What you do in here and tell me is private. I am not going to tell anyone else except if I am worried about you hurting yourself, hurting someone else, or being hurt by someone else. If one of these things might happen, I need to talk to another adult who can

make sure you are safe. If that ever happens, I will tell you what I am going to do.

Involvement of Others: Sometimes it helps more if your parents or teacher can do some things that might help you. Sometimes I set up a plan with kids that teachers keep track of in class so we can see what might help most. Other times it helps to meet with a kid and his parents together to see how everyone might help. If I am going to do this, I will let you know and discuss what I want to talk about with your teacher or parents. Do you have any questions?

AFFECTIVE ORIENTATION.
The affective component of the orientation involves the client's perception of the counselor as a likable, warm, trustworthy, and helpful person (yes, sort of like a Girl or Boy Scout). While these feelings really develop over time during the counseling process, the client's initial impression of the counselor is important. And this is something you can't really tell the client, but must convey to the client. The way to do this is by paying attention to and showing interest in the child. This is the purpose of the remainder of the first session.

DISCUSSING THE CHILD'S LIKES AND DISLIKES

I like to use a simple icebreaker activity I call, "My Favorite Things," to begin building rapport and getting to know a client. I have the child make a folder and then decorate the folder according to the topics I provide. The child may choose to draw or write her/his responses, arrange the responses anyway he/she desires, and add any additional decoration she/he wants. The materials I provide for this activity are an 11 by 17 inch sheet of construction paper or oaktag, pencils, crayons, and markers. I stay away from glitter and glue because these folders are used to store the child's art that is produced in counseling, thus, would be somewhat messy with those types of materials.

Topics used may be any of your choosing that would allow you to get to know the child better, but also be lighthearted. Some examples are provided below.
- Favorite food.
- Favorite activity.
- Favorite activity in school.
- Favorite television show or movie.
- Favorite book.
- Favorite place.
- Favorite class.
- A symbol that represents you.
- A self-portrait.

OBTAINING FAMILY INFORMATION

Obtaining family information is the third component of this pre counseling session. This is actually a very important activity, as it helps provide the counselor with information from the child's perspective which serves as part of the context for understanding the child's play. To accomplish this task, I have clients complete standard family drawings and, if capable, a genogram.

FAMILY DRAWINGS.
Family drawings are a traditional method for obtaining information regarding children's perceptions of their families, and themselves in relation to their families (Oster & Gould, 1987). I view this type of information as "soft data" about a child's experience that provides valuable information about how the child sees the world. It can provide an interesting perspective to consider, but cannot be viewed as definitive or even factual. It is a reflection of the client's perceptions which may or may not be based in reality.

With any type of drawing that is used for therapeutic or evaluative purposes, there are some important limitations to consider. First, the quality of drawings is influenced by children's level of cognitive functioning and developmental level (Koppitz, 1968). Before the age of eight, many characteristics of drawings that are commonly considered to be clinically significant, are influenced primarily by developmental factors (Koppitz). Second, individual characteristics of drawings cannot be considered to be significant by themselves. Drawing characteristics need to be viewed within the context of the entire drawing or series of drawings that a child completes. Consistency of characteristics across drawings can then be viewed as being more significant. Third, many elements of therapeutic drawings are simply common to drawings of most children in a particular age group (Naglieri, McNeish, & Bardos, 1991), and, thus, are of little significance as indicators of emotional conflict. For example, Williams (1996) found a small but significant correlation between some of the shading items on the DAP:SPED (Naglieri, McNeish, & Bardos) and elevated scores on depression and anxiety scales in a sample of third and fourth graders. However, adolescents commonly shade drawings, thus, assuming that shading is an indicator of either depression or anxiety for this group would be erroneous. Finally, therapeutic drawings are subject to the problem of eisegesis; that is, reading something into a drawing that we want to see. In other words, the observer imposes his or her perceptions of a situation onto the drawing (Kamphaus & Frick, 1996). It is important, then, for counselors and other clinicians to view drawings with a certain amount of skepticism, and to think about them within the context of other information that is known about children.

With these caveats in mind, why use drawings? Drawings are a familiar and developmentally appropriate activity for children. With younger children, who may not be able to provide clear and accurate information about their families through genograms, drawings may be the only way to obtain some information about how children see their families. I use two traditional family drawing techniques, the Draw-a Family or DAF (Appel, 1931; Wolff, 1942) and the Kinetic Family Drawing or KFD (Burns & Kaufmann, 1970). An example of the administration of these techniques is provided below.

EXAMPLE: Family Drawing Series
(Counselor presents the child with an 8 " X 11" sheet of white paper placed horizontally in front of the child, and a pencil.)

Counselor: I want you to draw a picture of your family for me.
Client: *Everyone?*
Counselor: You can include anyone you want, it's your drawing.
Client: *Should I draw myself?*
Counselor: That's up to you.
(Child completes family drawing. Counselor takes paper.)
(Counselor places second sheet of paper in front of the child as above.)
Counselor: Now, I want you to draw a picture of your family, including yourself, doing something together.
Client: *Can I make it baseball?*
Counselor: That's up to you, it's your drawing. Etc.

GENOGRAM
The next activity is the completion of a genogram. A genogram is a diagram of the client's family, which I introduce to the child as the child's family tree. The purpose of this activity is to obtain some insight into children's perceptions of their families. Basic guidelines, adapted from McGoldrick and Gerson (1985), for constructing a simple genogram are provided in Figure 5-1. An example of this activity is provided on the following page.

EXAMPLE

Counselor: What I would like to do now is draw your family tree. Do you know what a family tree is?
Client: No.
Counselor: It's a diagram or chart that shows who's in your family. Here are the rules. We show girls with circles and boys with squares. We'll start with your mom and dad. (Counselor draws parent portion of genogram.) What's your dad's name?
Client: Tom. (Counselor writes Tom on genogram.)
Counselor: What's your mom's name?
Client: Carol. (Counselor writes on genogram.)
Counselor: How old are your dad and mom?
Client: I think dad is 32 and mom is 34. (Counselor writes on genogram).
Counselor: Do you know what your father does for work?
Client: He drives 18-wheelers.
Counselor: So, he drives big rigs.
Client: Yeah. (Counselor writes this under father.)
Counselor: Does your mother work?
Client: Yeah, she works with road builders.
Counselor: What does she do?
Client: She drives bulldozers. (Counselor writes this in.)
Counselor: Now, are you the oldest, youngest or somewhere in the middle.
Client: I'm the oldest.
Counselor: Okay, so we are going to draw you right here. (Counselor draws on genogram.) And how old are you?
Client: Nine. (Counselor writes on genogram.)
Counselor: Would you like to do some of this diagram?
Client: Yeah.
Counselor: Okay, I'm going to let you draw in any brothers and sisters you have, the way I've drawn you in here. Who's next oldest?
Client: My sister, Taralynne.

FIGURE 5-1 SIMPLE GENOGRAM GUIDELINES

- Males: List age inside figure and name below the figure. List information about the individual below the name. (e.g., 12, John)
- Females
- Death of a Family Member (d. 1989, Cause of death.)
- Marital Relationship
- Non-marital Spousal Relationship
- Separation (s.5/97)
- Divorce (dv.9/98)
- Household: Enclose members within dotted line. Children listed chronologically.
- Identified Client

Counselor:	So, you draw a circle here and write her name and age here. What grade is Taralynne in?
Client:	*Third.*
Counselor:	Write that in here (counselor points under sister's circle). (Etc., until genogram is complete.)
Counselor:	Now I have an idea about who's in your family and how everyone fits together. Is there anything else you would like to add?
Client:	*My dog.*
Counselor:	Okay, why don't you draw a little picture of a dog right here. Then I am going to save your diagram in your folder, and I can use it in case I need to remember something about your family.

The completed genogram from this example is shown in Figure 5-2.

Smiths   **Jones**

⊠ d.1990 Farm accident.

(60s)

"Pop-pop" 60s Heart problems. Family lives down the road. Sees kids almost every day.

28 Aunt Suzie Very close to Jen.

"Nana" 50s Works in school cafe.

m.1982 dv.1984

34 Tom Truckdriver. Travels a lot. close to Jarad.

34 Carol Construction worker. Works late. Depends on Jen.

? Mike Married Carol at age 17. Div at 19. Childhood sweethearts.

9 Jennifer Gr.4 Worries about Mom.

8 Taralynne Gr.3 Gets along with Jen.

5 Jarad Pre-school Sisters take care of him.

FIGURE 5-2 JENNIFER'S GENOGRAM

GIVING THE CHILD THE OPPORTUNITY TO ASK QUESTIONS

I end the pre-counseling session by allowing the client to ask any questions they might have about the counseling situation or me. I sometimes also use drawing as a closure activity by asking the child to draw a picture of anything they want. Once this is done, I remind the child about the day and time I will see him or her for the first counseling session, then I end the pre-counseling session.

THE BEGINNING OF THE FIRST PLAY THERAPY SESSION

At the beginning of the first play therapy session, I remind the client about the rules we discussed in the pre-counseling session. If I am using the rule approach to limitsetting, I state the rules as described in Chapter 3. If I am using the situational approach, I simply tell the child that she or he may play with any of the toys and that I will let them know when time is up. From this point, the actual play therapy begins.

A WORD ABOUT GENERAL PRE-COUNSELING ORIENTATIONS

COUNSELOR ORIENTATION
For counselors who work in school settings, general orientations to counseling can be very helpful in paving the way for any future counseling that may occur. By general orientation, I mean providing information to groups of

children (such as classes) about counseling and the counselor, the assumption being that clients will emerge from these groups in the future. Just as with individual orientations, these general presentations can be broken down into cognitive (information about the counseling process) and affective (impressions of the counselor) orientations. The information provided in the cognitive orientation is similar to what was described above for the individual pre-counseling orientation. An example of this type of orientation from my own research (Cerio, 1989) is provided below.

EXAMPLE
(After entering the classroom, the counselor begins the session.)

Now I'm going to tell you about what I do. "Elementary school counselor" is a long name for the job I have, but it doesn't tell you what I do in my job. That's what I'm going to talk about and show you today. Specifically, I'm going to talk about the counseling part of my job.

"Counseling" is a word that means helping others solve their problems or feel better about something that bothers them. A counselor counsels – that is helps other people. An elementary school counselor helps children in his/her school.

Who does an elementary guidance counselor help?

(Pause, then call on anyone who raises his/her hand. Reflect responses, then summarize by continuing on.)

I help all kinds of children – normal kids like you, who are experiencing problems which are causing them to feel unhappy, angry, frustrated, frightened, uncomfortable, etc. In other words, I see kids who are experiencing unpleasant feelings about something. The children I see are not bad or crazy or anything like that. They are just people who need someone to help them figure things out.

What kinds of problems do children come to see me about?

(Pause and wait for students to respond, then continue on.)

There are many different kinds of problems that I help children solve. Some children come to me because they are having trouble getting along with other children. Some see me because they are having trouble with their schoolwork. Some are upset about something that has happened at home with someone in their family. Some children come to me simply because they feel bad – unhappy, angry, embarrassed, frustrated, etc. – and don't want to feel this way anymore.

How does an elementary school counselor help children solve their problems?

(Pause and wait for children to respond, repeating their answers. Then continue.)

The main way I do this is by listening to children when they come to me in my office, helping them understand their problems and their feelings about the problems, and then helping them figure out how to solve their problems. I don't tell kids how they should solve problems or that they are wrong for feeling a certain way. I just listen and work together with them helping them decide what to do. Counselors sometimes do other things besides just talking. A counselor might ask a child to draw a picture, make up a play with puppets, do an activity sheet, or just play with toys in the counselor's room. These are all ways that I help children solve problems.

How many times does a child have to see a counselor before a problem is solved? Does anyone want to guess?

(Pause for responses.)

You're all correct – it is not unusual for a child to see a counselor several times in order to solve a problem. Many times, counselors see children four, six or even twelve times before problems are solved. Remember, solving problems isn't necessarily easy and usually takes a lot of thinking and work by both the child and counselor. And...some children have big problems which they might not be able to solve. When this happens, the counselor will try to help the child think of ways to handle the problem better.

How long does a child spend with a counselor in a counseling session or meeting – five minutes, ten minutes, a half-hour? Does anyone want to guess?

(Pause, again, for responses.)

If you go to see your elementary school counselor, you will probably spend about a half-hour or an hour talking with him/her.

When a child talks to a counselor, whatever that child tells the counselor is a secret which the counselor cannot tell anyone else unless the child gives him or her permission to do so. However, solving problems isn't always easy, and sometimes, the problem cannot be solved by the child alone. There are times when a counselor needs to talk to a child's parents, teacher, or others in order to help the child. When this is the case, the counselor will let the child know that this is necessary and decide with the child what can be discussed with the other people involved. The only time that a counselor must talk to someone else about a child's secret is when the counselor thinks the child might get hurt. Confidentiality is the label given to the this rule about counselors keeping secrets.

If you want to see me the first thing you do is ask your teacher. He/She will give you a note or pass to see me or tell me that you want to see me if I'm not available on a particular day. If you want to come and see me, you should (outline the procedure a child has to follow in your school when voluntarily going to see the counselor.) My room is located by (or next to or across from)_____.

There might be times when your parents, teachers, or someone else in the school want you to see me. When this happens, I will let you know when I am going to see you and tell you why someone else thought talking to me might help you in some way.

AFFECTIVE ORIENTATION

Affective orientation is actually easier to accomplish within a general orientation approach. Remember, the affective orientation gives children an idea about who the counselor is and how she/he operates. It is an opportunity for counselors to convey that they like and value kids, and are warm and trustworthy. This can be accomplished through structured or unstructured activities. Structured activities include such things as classroom guidance or affective education programming in which the counselor meets on a regular basis with classes to cover counseling related topics such as understanding feelings, social skills, and other topics related to social-emotional functioning. Through these regular contacts with the counselor, children become more familiar with him or her as a person. An even less formal structured approach is meeting with classes to read age-appropriate books to them. Meeting this way three or four times with a particular class can be enough for kids to feel comfortable with the counselor.

Unstructured approaches include such activities as attending class parties, accompanying classes on field trips, or just standing in the hall and greeting children by name as they enter the school building. These simple situations convey to kids that the counselor cares enough to know their names and is more than just a person who lurks in some office and sees "bad" kids. It is a simple way to acknowledge children as persons.

Research supports the value of both cognitive and affective general orientations, demonstrating that children who are provided with a one session presentation on counseling understand the counseling process better than children who receive either no orientation or participate in non-informational activities with counselors. On the other hand, children who were involved in affective orientation activities indicated stronger preferences for the counselors involved in those activities than children who received either cognitive orientations or no orientation to counseling (Cerio, 1993). Finally, children who were involved in any type of group pre-counseling orientation were more likely to refer themselves for counseling than children who received no orientation (Cerio; Park & Williams, 1984). Thus, it would seem that a small bit of work, such as meeting with each classroom at the beginning of the school year for a short orientation to counseling, could pay great benefits in terms of counselor effectiveness.

Homework

Outline information you might provide children about counseling, your professional role, and you as a person, as part of your own pre-counseling orientation activity. You might think about whether or not you want to use a more novel or interesting form of presentation, for instance, a puppet show for younger children, or videotaped examples for older children. Jot down your ideas below.

_____

_____

_____

_____

_____

_____

_____

_____

Chapter 6

Use of Games in Play Therapy

Homework

Before starting this chapter, obtain the games listed below and play each of them for at least 15 minutes with your partner. Complete the self-evaluation form and continue reading. You will want to refer back to your self-assessment as you progress through the chapter.

Candyland
Chutes n' Ladders
Memory
Connect Four
Trouble

Sorry
Battleship
Uno
Cards (Go-Fish, War)
Checkers

Play Session Self Assessment

1. With which games did you feel most comfortable? Why?

2. With which games did you feel most uncomfortable? Why?

3. Did you experience any particular thoughts in relation to certain game activities (memories, visualizations, etc.)?

   Play Activity   Thought

4. Did you experience any strong feelings in relation to certain game activities?

   Play Activity   Feeling

5. List any questions you have about games at this point.

Usefulness of Games in Play Therapy

Using games in therapy – specifically board games – is one of the areas of ongoing debate in the play therapy field. Traditional child-centered therapists view board games as detrimental to the therapeutic process, eschewing the use of such materials (Landreth, 1991). They view games as interfering with the spontaneity and creativity of children's play, as imposing unnecessary rules on the counseling situation, and as fostering competitiveness, which they see as counterproductive to therapy. Others, such as Schaefer and Reid (1986), argue that games are a normal part of children's everyday experience and, thus, can serve as useful tools in play therapy. Certainly, including games in the playroom adds another dimension to the therapeutic process and expands the age range of play therapy to include middle and late childhood, particularly when working with kids who are functioning at the chronologically appropriate developmental level.

What do games bring to the playroom? As opponents of games point out, one of the primary factors that games introduce to the playroom is rules. While purists see this as negative, more eclectic practitioners (including me), see these rules as providing metaphors for the outside world. Children are expected to follow rules outside of the playroom, and most of these rules are not changeable. When a rule is violated, there are consequences. Games incorporate similar expectations, albeit with more benign consequences. But games have many other functions in the playroom.

Games provide structure. Some children simply cannot tolerate the more unstructured format of the playroom. The relative openness of the tasks and the responsibility to make choices produces anxiety that can sometimes be overwhelming for these children. The rules and goals of games provide predictability and limited choices that reduce task demand and, subsequently, anxiety. This allows children to ease into the play routine until they are comfortable with less structured tasks.

Games provide a useful template for transference. Games played between child and therapist provide excellent opportunities to utilize the client's parent/adult authority figure transference reaction. Within the structure of games, kids can safely discharge negative feelings and conflicts they experience toward adults. This is related to the next two functions of games.

Games introduce both competition and cooperation into the therapy. Competition is not necessarily a bad thing to introduce into the therapeutic situation. It is the type of competition that is important, not competition itself. Competition that occurs in the context of traditional board games is a type that places child and therapist on an equal footing. That is, the child is just as likely to win the game as the adult is. This means that the child has the unique opportunity to get the better of an adult, something that seldom occurs in the child's everyday life. Since most of the kids I work with have problematic relationships with adults in their lives (parents, teachers, principals), being able to compete with and beat the therapist allows the child to discharge negative feelings towards other adults in the child's life. That is, competition becomes a tool for transference.

Interestingly enough, games also provide opportunities for cooperation between child and counselor. I see this occurring in situations where the child doesn't know how to play a game or doesn't understand the strategy of the game. In these cases, I, in effect, play on the child's side, helping the child understand alternatives and decide on moves. The game, then, becomes a cooperative effort to beat me.

Games allow for safe discharge of aggression. The design of board games makes them wonderful tools for allowing children to express anger within a structured and emotionally safe context. This, again, is especially useful with children who have difficult relationships with adults in their lives. There is nothing more satisfying for some of the kids with whom I work than sending me back to start in Trouble or giving me card after card of "draw fours" while playing Uno. In this way, a child can "get back at" and frustrate an adult who represents other adults in the child's life.

EXAMPLE:
Counselor and child are playing Uno together.
Counselor: Whatever you do, don't give me any "Draw 2" or "Draw 4" cards. (Sets up transference possibilities.)
Child: (Puts down a "Draw 2"). There, I got you. (Then puts down another "Draw 2.") Got you again. (Then puts down a "Draw 4" and laughs.) You're never going to win.
Counselor: You're killing me. I'm never going to win this game.

Games serve as both assessments of and interventions for frustration tolerance. Did you ever become so upset while playing a game that you just wanted to tip the board over? A common element of traditional board games is that they include a measure of frustration. Thus, games provide excellent opportunities for counselors to assess how their clients deal with frustration. Difficulties with frustration tolerance are manifested in behaviors ranging from the "board tipping" described above to a child simply refusing to continue with a game when she begins losing. These types of situations provide the therapist with insight into the child's self-esteem, identity, and coping skills. Based on this assessment, I use games to model coping skills and help the child build tolerance to frustration. This procedure is described later in this chapter.

Games provide necessary emotional distance at certain points in the therapy. Sometimes kids simply need down time from the emotional stimulation of play therapy. Games allow kids to do this by allowing them to refocus from an emotionally charged play activity to the task requirements of a game. This gives the child time to pull back and "recharge the batteries," especially when the child feels overwhelmed by uncomfortable emotions. Typically, the child returns to more unstructured, metaphorical play once she feels calm and relaxed. In this way, games actually act as soothing devices for children in play therapy.

EXAMPLE

A 6-year-old boy whose parents are divorcing becomes involved in playing out a scenario in which a puppy is yelling at the "daddy" dog, "You are a very bad daddy. Go away!" After repeating this several times, the boy has the puppy turn to the "mommy" dog and yell, "And you are a very bad mommy. You go away, too!" The boy pauses for a few seconds then asks the counselor, "Can we play a game?" The boy plays a game with the counselor for a few minutes, then returns to unstructured play.

Games provide opportunities for the therapist to meet a child's needs for nurturance. A very simple way I use games is to communicate that I will take care of the child's needs within the context of the game. Opportunities to do this occur when the child is getting bad rolls of the dice in a game like Trouble or drawing unhelpful cards in games like Sorry or Uno. In these cases, I give the child a "gift" by allowing him to use one of my moves, or by giving him a useful card. This serves as a small way to communicate to the child that I am there to help him and not just to win a game.

EXAMPLE

A counselor and child play Sorry together. The counselor keeps drawing the cards necessary to move players out onto the board, while the child does not. The child shows signs of frustration and discouragement.

Counselor: This has to be really frustrating for you. I've been really lucky and you can't seem to get the right cards. I'll tell you what. I'm going to give you this card so you can get started. Maybe it will change your luck. Anyway, it's not much fun for me to play and not have anyone I can send back to start (sets up transference possibilities).

Typology of Games

There is a logic and developmental progression in the design of common board games. Games can be classified on a continuum from ones that rely primarily on luck in order to win, to those that rely primarily on skill. As one would expect, games designed for younger children fall on the luck end of this continuum, while those for older children require skill and understanding of strategy. Figure 6-1 at right provides some examples of this typology of games.

In general younger children tend to choose games such as Candyland and Chutes n' Ladders, which rely on drawing the cards or spinning a spinner to progress on the board. Middle childhood games like Trouble, Sorry, and Uno incorporate a combination of luck and skill. In Sorry, the child not only needs to be lucky enough to select helpful cards, but also needs to choose the strategic alternatives described on the cards that will help the child reach "home" more quickly. Games that are geared more toward late childhood include chess and Monopoly, which require much more intentional use of strategy (and maybe a little bit of luck).

The type of games that a particular child chooses consistently, provides some insight into where the child falls on this continuum. For instance, a younger child might try to play chess or Trouble but, finding the task demands too difficult, moves to Chutes n' Ladders. More significant are older children who have difficulty with frustration tolerance and such low self esteem that even falling behind in a game is hurtful. It is not unusual for kids with these problems to begin playing an age-appropriate game, such as Sorry, then, feeling that they are going to lose, quit the game and move to a developmentally lower level game, such as Candyland. These are the types of children that I target for the frustration tolerance building procedure described below.

In these cases, I manipulate the game as a therapeutic intervention. I *do* advocate losing on purpose, as long as it is therapeutically useful

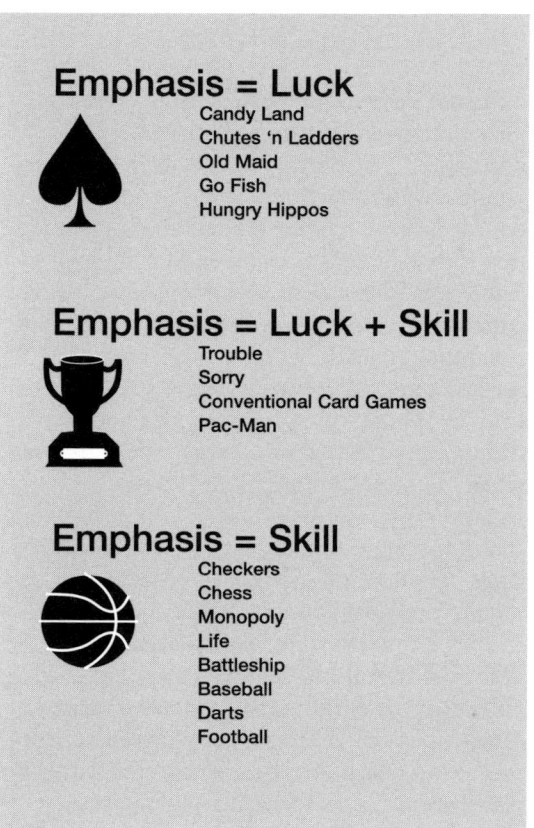

Figure 6-1 Typology of Games

and not obvious enough to insult a child's intelligence. As an adult, I should be skilled enough to do this in a covert manner so as not to be discovered by the child. I begin the procedure by making poor moves and acting as if I am not paying attention to how my moves might hinder my progress. This typically allows the child to win fairly decisively. I then begin making better moves so that the outcomes of the games get closer, but the child still wins. While doing this, I use externalized self-talk, so the child can hear the frustration I am experiencing and how I am coping with it.

EXAMPLE
(Counselor speaking) Oh nuts, I just moved this there and now you have to send me back to start. I'm getting killed! Oh well, it's only a game, and I will have a chance to beat you next time.

I then play the game to win (if I can) and beat the child. I encourage him to use the self-talk that I used to cope with losing, and reinforce this when it occurs. If the child still displays difficulty in losing, I return to the middle part of the procedure (losing but making it close) and continue from there.

STRUCTURE OF GAMES

Traditional board games incorporate certain common elements in their structure. If you have altogether too much time on your hands and a relatively uninteresting life, as I do, it might be worth looking at a number of these games and noticing some of these elements. For instance, it is not unusual for the playing area to be made up of a trail or path of some kind that contains a number of spaces divisible by four (80, 100, etc.). There usually is a short-cut to winning that can be taken based on a lucky draw or on understanding the strategy of moving a certain way. There are also delays which slow players' progress, such as "Molasses Swamp" in Candyland, or drawing a "Sorry" card in Sorry. In this way, frustration, anticipation, and a sense of achievement or victory are incorporated into the normal structure of the game.

Interestingly enough, this logic in game construction usually allows the progress in a board game to remain close when only two players are playing. Winning typically comes down to both players being near the ultimate goal and waiting for the right card or roll of the dice. Thus, if the counselor does nothing to manipulate the progress of a game, it will more likely than not be a close competition with a child, providing many opportunities to model frustration tolerance skills.

CHEATING

One of the big questions from my students is, "What do I do if a child cheats?" This is a tough one because cheating is a betrayal of trust, the foundation building block of a therapeutic relationship. Cheating is a specific type of limitsetting situation, albeit, a delicate one, which must be handled appropriately because of the potential repercussions to the relationship.

The first rule in a cheating situation is don't ignore it. If you see a child do something that is against the rules of a game, you need to attend to it. However, how you attend to it is critical. DON'T automatically accuse the child of cheating. I remember walking down the hall of a clinic in which I worked and overhearing one of our clinicians yelling at a child, "You cheated!" The child then yelled back, "No I didn't!" And a power struggle ensued. THIS IS NOT THERAPEUTICALLY USEFUL.

First, point out to the child that she has done something against the rules and find out why. It is not unusual for children to learn to play games differently at home because parents sometimes change the rules. In these cases, it is important to clarify the rules that the child has learned at home and to agree to either play by these rules or the standard rules. Sometimes kids seem to be cheating because of simple skill deficits. For instance, young children will miscount spaces they are supposed to move because they tend to count the space they are on as "one." This results in their moving one space less than they are supposed to. In these situations, play with the child and help them count spaces. If they move the wrong number of spaces, don't be afraid to correct them. In card games, if they shuffle or deal cards incorrectly, again, help them – work with them.

The most difficult type of cheating is when a child blatantly tries to do something to make sure he wins, such as stacking the cards to get a winning hand. When this occurs, I approach it as a limitsetting situation using the I A-C-T model. I INTERRUPT the behavior by taking time out from the game. I ACKNOWLEDGE the child's need to cheat and possible feelings connected with this need. I COMMUNICATE the limit, usually referring to the game rules. And I TARGET alternatives, again referring to game rules. Some examples of this are provided below.

EXAMPLE 1

Counselor: Time out (Interrupt). Looks like you want to change the rules (Acknowledge behavior), but the rules of the game are clear and have to be followed (Communicate the limit). If you want to play this game, we have to play by the rules, but if you want to play it differently, we can discuss new rules after we are done and try following those rules when we play next time (Target an alternative).

Child: *But my parents taught me to play it differently.*

Counselor: I'll tell you what. Let's stop the game here, and you tell me the rules that your parents use. Then we will start the game over and play by those rules. But you have to remember that once we start, the rules won't change.

EXAMPLE 2

(Counselor speaking) Let's stop for a minute (I). It looks like you are really worried (or upset) about losing, so you want to change the rules (A). But the game has rules and you are not allowed to change them while you are playing (C). Let's continue playing and see how the game turns out this time. Then, we can talk about different rules (T).

EXAMPLE 3

(Counselor speaking) I have to tell you that I've seen you move those extra spaces two times now (I). And I am really concerned that you are worried that you won't win (A). We can't change the rules (C), so I am going to ask you to trust me and see how the game turns out. Maybe I can even help you with some moves so you will understand some of the tricks to winning this game (T).

One belief of mine that might be evident is that cheating is related to a problem with the child's trust of the therapist. A child feels a need to cheat because he does not believe that the therapist will meet the child's need – that is, the child has not developed a sense of what Erikson (1963) termed basic trust. Thus, I think that it is up to the therapist to demonstrate to the child that the therapist understands this and will indeed meet the child's need – in this case, the child's need is to not feel bad about himself. If the counselor succeeds in doing this, the child will no longer need to cheat because losing a game will not be damaging to the child's self-esteem.

As you also might have noticed, I do not believe in changing rules once a game is being played. One of the reasons for including games in the playroom is because games provide direct metaphors to the rules the child encounters in her everyday life. Rules can't be changed at a whim in the real world and the child has to deal with the consequences when she chooses to break a rule. Similarly, the child needs to deal with the consequences of rules in games. However, if there is a good rationale for changing a rule before we start playing a game, I am open to negotiating this with the agreement that once we start playing the game, the rules don't change. The big thing to keep in mind when cheating occurs is to use the situation as a therapeutic moment, and to not get caught up in a power struggle.

THERAPEUTIC GAMES

I have said little about therapeutic games up to this point for one important reason. I don't particularly like this type of game because it tends to be unreal. That is, therapeutic games are not a common part of kids' lives outside the playroom, and these games have specific purposes that are fairly narrow. The purpose of most of these games is to generate discussion about a specific topic, be it feelings, social skills, conflict resolution, anger management, divorce, or a myriad of other counseling related topics. Thus, the purpose is not play but talk and skill development.

In spite of these misgivings, I do see therapeutic games as being useful at certain points of the play therapy process, and for certain types of counseling activities, such as theme-oriented groups. One useful function of therapeutic games is to move the therapy beyond a roadblock or resistance. These games provide a structure for discussion which sometimes helps clients relax and focus on specific questions or issues. This helps reduce resistance and typically leads to more open discussion with the therapist.

A second function of therapeutic games is for intervening later in the counseling process. Thus, if a child has certain skill deficits, introducing a game that focuses on development of those skills can provide opportunities for skill training, modeling, practice, and feedback from the therapist.

Given the two functions described above, it is not surprising that therapeutic games are also useful in theme-oriented groups for generating discussion among members. As previously stated, these games impose a structure and focus for discussions which provide reasonable limits on emotional risk-taking. The games also allow students to choose not to share, and do inject some fun into the discussion format.

An actual downside of therapeutic games is that they usually eliminate competition from the game structure. That is, there are no winners or losers in the game. These games are structured so that everyone wins if everyone else meets the goal of the game, or so there is really no end to the game. This is the element that kids often find frustrating. Many of these games are aimed at middle childhood stage children, and children at this stage like competing because they are working on "mastery" developmental tasks. Thus, the lack of competition in therapeutic games reduces some of the interest value for these children.

There are literally hundreds of therapeutic games being marketed today. You can buy a therapeutic game for almost any counseling situation. The question for me is, do I really need to? Games are relatively easy to create, and I have found it fun and challenging to develop games that meet the specific needs of my job setting. For example, when I was working with a group of children who had discipline problems in a school, I developed a game that used that school as its setting. The characters in the game were teachers and administrators in the school. The rules were taken from the school rules. The consequences were based on consequences the children had experienced in the school. Knowing the structure of games I described above, it is relatively simple to design a customized therapeutic game that costs little, and is more relevant to the clients with whom it is being used.

In addition to creating your own therapeutic games, you can adapt common board games to specific therapeutic goals (Nickerson & O'Laughlin, 1983). For instance, one time I was working with a pre-adolescent boy who liked to play checkers. We would play checkers almost the entire session. But whenever I pointed out a feeling the boy was expressing, he would shut down and not talk. Since one of the reasons the boy was seeing me was to discuss feelings related to his parents' divorce, I decided to change the rules of our checkers games so that this goal could be facilitated within the context of the game. I made a deck of cards on which I wrote questions about feelings, personal preferences, and family issues. I then instituted a rule that before a player could move, he had to answer a question drawn from the deck by the other player. This meant that both the boy and I had to disclose information about ourselves. This had the effect I hoped, helping the client open up, but also giving him some control by allowing him to ask me questions. We eventually stopped using the deck and agreed to answer any questions asked by the other person, which helped the boy begin discussing his feelings about his family situation. I have used adaptations with other games, such as putting numbers at certain locations of the Trouble board which corresponded to theme cards, and having the colors of Candyland cards correspond to discussion topics. Using traditional board games for structured therapeutic purposes simply requires that the counselor be a little creative and flexible.

Summary

Despite misgivings by more traditional child-centered play therapists about including games in the therapeutic environment, games provide useful alternatives to less structured play therapy. My hope is that, from the information provided in this chapter, you have developed some sense of the variety of uses for games. The trick is, to coin a term used by one of my professors, to not be "functionally fixed." That is, don't get stuck on the primary goal of the game. Rather, think about how the playing of the game is therapeutically useful, and be open to adapting games to the needs of the therapy.

Homework

Assuming that you have tried out some of the common games used in play therapy, it is now time to practice responding therapeutically to game play. You are to complete at least one simulation with your partner role playing a child who is playing games in therapy. During this simulation, you should respond to the client's moves and conversation using the facilitative responding skills. Your partner should also be sure to include some limitsetting situations within the context of the games. Before beginning, be sure that you are familiar with the rules for each game you are using. Complete the self assessment when you are done.

PLAY SESSION SELF ASSESSMENT

1. With which games did you feel most comfortable? Why?

2. With which games did you feel most uncomfortable? Why?

3. Did you experience any particular thoughts in relation to certain games (memories, visualizations, etc.)?

   Play Activity   Thought

4. Did you experience any strong feelings in relation to certain games?

   Play Activity   Feeling

5. What limitsetting situations occurred, and how did you respond to them?

6. List any questions you have about games at this point.
   Limitsetting Situation   Response

7. Rate your comfort level with using games in play therapy.

         1   2   3   4   5   6   7
   Very Uncomfortable   Very Comfortable

Chapter 7

Therapist's Role

What is a Play Therapist

Now that you have an idea of basic responding, you are ready to be a play therapist, right? Wrong! Being a counselor or therapist is more than just providing a certain type of response. Given the sophistication of desk top computers today, even one of those machines can be programmed to provide appropriate responses through voice synthesizers. But think of that idea. What a voice synthesizer lacks is emotional content, warmth, and genuine concern for the individual. It is these non-specific variables that make a counselor a counselor. The responses are simply a means to an end: the creation of a therapeutic context or relationship in which a client can feel free to explore the meaning of experience, problemsolve, and develop and test coping strategies. This is the essence of the therapist's role in play therapy and counseling in general.

There are a number of things to consider in addition to how you respond to children's play, if you desire to be an effective play therapist. Among these are your attitudes toward children, your belief system or "creed" as a helping person, your many roles in life, and your personal style. These not only influence your position as a therapist, but also will determine what kind of play therapy you use, or if you choose not to utilize play therapy at all.

A Matter of Attitude

At this point, it is time to do some self-reflection. What do you believe about children? Should they be seen and not heard? Are they sugar and spice and everything nice? Take a few minutes and complete the questionnaire on the next page. Think about how you think and feel about children as you do this.

Directions: Rate each statement to reflect how you really feel, based on the following scale:
1 = Strongly Disagree
2 = Disagree
3 = Agree
4 = Strongly Agree

___ 1. Children should be treated with the same respect as adults.
___ 2. Children should be allowed to do as they please.
___ 3. Children are not able to make reasonable decisions.
___ 4. Children should be seen and not heard.
___ 5. Children should be free to be themselves.
___ 6. Children and adults should be on equivalent levels in a hierarchy.
___ 7. It is important to set clearly defined limits for children.
___ 8. Children should be treated with respect.
___ 9. It is up to adults to make things better for children.
___ 10. Children need to know that some rules are unchangeable.
___ 11. Children cannot be expected to be responsible.
___ 12. Children's problems are usually products of their parents' problems.
___ 13. Children need to learn to respect authority.
___ 14. Children are not capable of solving their own problems.
___ 15. A child's problem usually signals the existence of a problem in another family member.

Now, review your responses and think about what they reflect about you. Do you tend to be more laissez faire with children? Do you feel a need to fix things for kids? Do you think kids need to know their place with adults? After looking over your responses, summarize your attitude toward children in a few sentences below.

_____
_____
_____
_____
_____
_____
_____
_____
_____
_____
_____
_____
_____
_____
_____
_____
_____

Developing Your Creed

Just as important as your attitudes toward children is your philosophy of counseling. That is, what do you believe about therapy? What do you think the therapist's position should be? The client's position? Can people choose to change, or do they need to be changed by others? Is the client the person with a problem or just reacting to a system with a problem? Should the therapist focus on problems or solutions? These are all important and relevant questions that counselors need to ask themselves, and especially important questions when working with children. Since children usually do not choose to seek help themselves, but are referred by adults, counselors need to have a clear idea about their beliefs about working with such involuntary clients.

My good friend, Gunner, whom I mentioned in Chapter One, wrote what he called his "counselor's creed," many years ago (Gunnison, 1975). His intention was to communicate to his clients what his belief system was concerning counseling and the capacity for human beings to change. This creed, which has been reprinted many times over the years, is a series of statements which clearly delineates Gunner's philosophy to clients. It is also a living document which has changed since its first publication, reflecting changes in Gunner's belief system and approach to counseling. Read his example of a counselor's creed on the following page.

Creed of a Counselor

1. I will not agree to help you go off the edge. I will not agree to help you become a robotized normal and adjusted person. I will not help you stay and wallow in the cesspool of your own making. All of these go against my values. I will help you to grow, to become more productive by your own definition. I will help you to become more autonomous, more resistant to enculturation, more loving of yourself, more excited, sensitive, and full, more free to continue becoming the authority for your own living.
2. I cannot give you your dreams or "fix you up," simply because I cannot.
3. I cannot make you grow or grow for you. You must grow for yourself.
4. I cannot take away your loneliness or pain.
5. I will not sense your world for you, evaluate your world for you, or tell you what is best for you in your world, for you have your own world.
6. I cannot convince you of the crucial choice of choosing the scary uncertainty of growing over the safe misery of not growing.
7. I want to be with you and know you as a rich and growing friend, yet I cannot get close to you when you choose not to grow.
8. When I begin to care for you out of pity, when I begin to lose trust in you, then I am toxic, bad, and inhibiting for you, and you for me.
9. [I] BELIEVE that [I] cannot help you if you CHOOSE NOT to help yourself. [I] have to TRUST YOUR COMMITMENT to ACT, to CHANGE, and to GROW.
10. If you can accept all of this, then perhaps we can help each other. (Gunnison, 1999, pp. 283-284)

Since Gunner works primarily with adults, his creed is designed for that client group in relation to his belief system. Yet many of his beliefs are still relevant to any type of counseling because they highlight Gunner's foundation in Roger's (1961) Person-Centered approach. Virginia Axline, a pioneer in the play therapy field and a protegé of Carl Rogers proposed what could now be called a creed in her Eight Principles (Axline, 1947). These principles apply directly to play therapists and their work with children. They also demonstrate Axline's roots in the Person-Centered approach. I have paraphrased these Eight Principles below. Read them and think about your own beliefs about children and therapy.

Axline's Eight Principles

1. Establish a warm and friendly relationship.
2. Accept the child as he or she is.
3. Establish a feeling of permissiveness.
4. Recognize and reflect feelings.
5. Respect the child's ability to solve problems.
6. Don't direct the child's actions.
7. Trust the process.
8. Establish limits which provide an anchor to reality.

These two creeds are personal statements of two therapists that may or may not apply to you. I offer them to you as examples only. The important next step for you is to formulate your own creed of counseling. In doing this, keep in mind that your creed is a living document that will change as you change. The quantity and type of experience you have, additional training, your family situation, and even your age will affect your creed over time. You might even find your creed changing as you progress through the reading and exercises presented in this book. It is all part of the process. Now, take some time and begin to outline your basic beliefs regarding children and therapy in the space provided in the next column.

My Counselor's Creed

_____
_____
_____
_____
_____
_____
_____
_____
_____
_____
_____
_____
_____
_____
_____
_____
_____
_____
_____
_____
_____
_____
_____
_____
_____
_____

The Therapist's Role

What does the play therapist actually do besides reflect the child's actions or verbalizations? I see the counselor in play therapy as being similar to that of a coach. Coaches watch their players perform, make comments, give advice to improve performance, demonstrate, sometimes play along with the players, and evaluate progress. This, in a nutshell, is what the counselor does in play therapy. Some of the distinguishing characteristics of the play therapist are listed below. As you review these, you should develop a sense of my counselor's creed as it applies to play therapy.

The play therapist is stable and predictable. Children need to have a clear sense of who the counselor is and how he/she will react. The play therapist provides this by being calm, accepting, and consistent in the way she responds to children over time. This allows children to feel safe in expressing themselves through their play.

The play therapist utilizes the SKILLED skills to develop the therapeutic conditions that facilitate change. Many years ago, Carl Rogers described a group of "non-specific" factors which he called the "necessary conditions for change" in psychotherapy (Rogers, 1957). These factors which I called PEGS in Chapter One--unconditional positive regard, empathy, genuineness, and specificity of response--form the foundation of the therapeutic relationship. And it is the relationship that drives the therapy, whether you are using non-directive or directive approaches. The SKILLED responding format is simply a method for helping counselors develop a therapeutic relationship with their clients in play therapy. Hence, it is important for the counselor to convey PEGS by attending and responding to the child's play.

The play therapist allows the child to fulfill his need for a nurturing relationship, while encouraging autonomy and initiative. Whether non-directive or directive in approach, play therapists become significant adult caregivers to their child clients. In this role, it is important that counselors provide an affectionate relationship which conveys unconditional positive regard. In doing so, the therapist needs to balance the child's dependency needs with the developmental drive to be independent and take initiative. In practice, this involves soothing children when they are upset, encouraging children to do things when they doubt their capacities, and providing opportunities for children to make decisions during sessions.

The play therapist insures the child's emotional and physical safety. It is as important for children to have structured, stable, and predictable environments, as it is to have a stable and predictable play therapist. Thus, the play therapist provides this by maintaining standard play room organization, establishing rules or limits that are clear to the child, and not allowing the child to become so overstimulated that the child feels out of control.

The play therapist respects the child's right to choose. Children exist in a world in which their lives are almost completely controlled by adults, either directly or indirectly. The playroom is a unique place where most of these rules are suspended for that short period of time that is the play session. It is the play therapist's task to provide opportunities to make choices, whether it is a limitsetting situation or simply a choice of what color to use in a drawing. This principle applies to both non-directive and directive approaches to play therapy. While the importance of allowing choice is the same, the manner and types of choices will differ between these two approaches.

The play therapist participates with the child when appropriate. A question that beginning play therapists often ask me is, "Should I play with the client?" Traditional child-centered play therapists typically do not involve themselves in the child's play. They observe and respond to the child's play but maintain the observer position to avoid directing the child's play in any way.

But I have found that children want to engage me, and playing with me is a very effective way to do this. Thus, during exploratory and working through stages of the process, I play with children *when they invite me to do so*. I allow the client to direct the play as much as possible to avoid injecting my own ideas into the child's world. So, if a child is pretending and wants me to play a character, I ask the child to tell me what I am supposed to do, how I am supposed to respond, and so forth. If a child wants to play a game, I allow the child to choose the game, pick my game piece or color, and decide who goes first.

During the later stage of the process when I may be implementing specific interventions, I sometimes initiate interactive play with the child as part of an intervention. For instance, if I want to model a coping skill for a child, I might create a "pretend" using puppets in which the child has to formulate strategies to respond to situations she encounters outside of the playroom. Or, I might tell the child a story that provides a useful metaphor that is designed to help the child deal with a particular issue. Or, I might take time out from the play situation to teach the child a specific skill, such as a relaxation technique. These are a few examples of more prescriptive play that is therapist directed.

The play therapist enjoys the child and is appropriately playful. While being a counselor is a job, this doesn't mean that one has to be deadly serious all of the time. Humor and fun are great medicine, and play is a naturally fun activity. Play therapists should have fun with their clients, laugh with them, tease them affectionately, and enjoy their time with their clients. Children easily recognize adults who genuinely like them and the time they spend with them. Yet, counselors must also be prepared for times when the play is not fun for the child, when it stimulates unpleasant feelings and memories that are upsetting to the child. At these times, the therapist needs to shift to a caretaking role in which she metaphorically cleans and bandages the child's emotional brush burn. This requires constant awareness of what is going on with the child, both externally and internally.

The play therapist tailors the approach to the child's problem and utilizes the client's resources in developing interventions. My approach to play therapy does not espouse a "one size fits all" philosophy. Instead, I feel that it is important to incorporate techniques into the therapy that will be more useful with a particular problem and with a particular child's resources. While I use a more non-directive, child-centered approach earlier in the therapeutic process, I will integrate other approaches that I see as being helpful after I have developed a clear understanding of the child's issues, feelings, and skill deficits. So, with one child, I may elect to continue using a non-directive approach. With another, I may use modeling and behavior contracts. With a third, I might shift to mutual storytelling. These decisions are driven by the child's and not the counselor's needs. This type of approach also requires a broad background in a variety of therapeutic systems and techniques, which places much responsibility on the counselor to continually educate and develop herself as a professional.

The play therapist is firm and consistent in setting limits. The establishment of limits is a necessary part of providing a predictable environment. Thus, play therapists need to be sure to set clear limits, and follow through consistently in enforcing these limits.

The play therapist respects the child's right to privacy. As I stated above, children exist in an adult world, and part of this reality is that children have very little privacy. Part of the uniqueness of the playroom is that children are allowed to maintain their privacy within certain limits. So, if a child chooses to not talk about something, the play therapist respects this and does not force the child to talk. Products of the child's play such as drawings or clay figures are not placed on display for other children to see. To do so would be analogous to offering a transcript or playing an audiotape of an adult client's counseling session to another client.

The most difficult aspect of this principle is that parents are not given direct information about the child's play unless the child gives permission to do so. As previously stated, there are some limits to this. Specifically, if a child says or does something that causes concern about the child's safety, or about the child endangering someone, this information is communicated to appropriate adults. However, the counselor should inform the child about these limitations to privacy, using age-appropriate language, at the outset of therapy. The child should consequently be reminded about these limitations should a situation arise in which information must be disclosed. Outside of these limitations, any information communicated to parents is offered as the counselor's general impressions of the child's therapy.

The play therapist recognizes the effect of transference and countertransference on the therapeutic process. Transference is a psychoanalytic construct that refers to a process in which the client transfers issues, conflicts, and feelings to the therapist (Arlow, 1989). In the traditional sense, these conflicts are related to unresolved pre-oedipal issues--that is, issues from early childhood (Arlow). However, the term transference has been bandied about recently in a more general sense to describe any conflicts, emotions, or issues that the client brings into the therapy room from outside the therapy room. Using this definition, transference can occur related to recent events, such as problems at work or with a spouse, or even something like not being able to find a parking space near the counselor's office. The important element of transference is that the client directs her feelings toward the therapist AS IF the therapist is the actual target of the conflict.

Countertransference involves the same process in the opposite direction. That is, countertransference is the process of the therapist bringing in issues, conflicts, and the like to the therapy room, and reacting to the client AS IF the client is the actual target of these feelings (Levy, 1984). This can result in inappropriate responses to the client which at best are not therapeutically useful, and at worse might be damaging.

Because of the nature of the adult and child positions in play therapy, transference and countertransference are factors about which the counselor must be keenly aware. There is an automatic power differential between therapist and child that results in some routine transference and countertransference situations. The most common of these is that of parental or adult authority figure transference and countertransference. In these situations, the child reacts to the therapist as the child does to her parents and/or the therapist reacts to the child as a parent rather than a therapist. Transference and countertransference are discussed in depth later in this book.

The play therapist allows for the possibility of regression and uses this to enhance the therapeutic process. Play is an activity that allows children to explore their needs within the context of fantasy. Because of the unique client-counselor relationship in play therapy, children often feel comfortable enough to engage in regressive behavior: that is, behaviors that are more characteristic of younger children. This may manifest itself in such ways as a nine- or ten-year-old using baby talk, a seven-year-old wanting to nurse from a baby bottle, or an eight-year-old wanting to be rocked like a baby. Regressive behaviors are common ways that children communicate and attempt to satisfy emotional needs. In play therapy, IT IS VERY IMPORTANT TO ALLOW CHILDREN TO EXPRESS THESE NEEDS within certain reasonable limits. The weight of responsibility rests on the counselor's shoulders to become comfortable with regressive play, and to NOT inhibit such play because of the counselor's discomfort (a good example of countertransference).

The play therapist understands the impact of the child's family system on the therapeutic process. Children do not exist in a vacuum. Their lives are constantly influenced by the adults and institutions around them, be it parents, teachers, religious groups, or social service agencies. It is incumbent upon the play therapist to recognize and understand the larger system in which the child functions, and to intervene if necessary and possible. Otherwise, working with a child individually, and isolated from this larger system, may prove to be totally fruitless if system factors are such that they maintain the child's symptoms.

The play therapist is a patient observer who thinks about the child's metaphors within the context of the child's everyday experience. This principle is the product of all the beliefs and behaviors stated above. It is the essence of what I do as a practitioner of play therapy. I observe, I describe, I label feelings, I watch for repetitive themes and patterns, and I think about how a particular theme reflects what is going on in the child's life. The play of the angry little boy whose mother just had a baby takes on new meaning when the little boy continually buries and unburies a baby doll in the sandbox. So, too, does the play of the little girl whose parents are involved in a custody battle, when she tips over the dollhouse and says, "The father started it on fire," each time she enters the playroom.

While some play therapy approaches rely on common or universal interpretations, this type of approach does not. Instead, the counselor must have a sense of each child's unique context, and to do this, the counselor must have access to background information about the child. This includes information about the problem, the child's family and school experiences, and developmental history. Only then can the counselor have a firm sense of how the child's play relates to the child's experience.

It is important to understand that this is an internal process of the therapist. My understanding of the child's play is not shared with the child as an interpretation. Instead, I respond within the child's metaphor, using the child's language. Taking the example from above, when the girl stated, "The father started the house on fire," I responded, "So the dad started the house on fire," staying with the generic "the" before "dad." In this way, I respect the distance that the child places between the metaphor and her real experience, while at the same time understanding the child's subtext to be, "My parents are wrecking my family and I'm mad as hell."

Summary

If you think about the role I have defined for the therapist, in its simplest terms it is the role of the "Good Mother," using the term mother in a gender-free manner. The Good Mother is nurturing, predictable, understanding, playful, consistent, and firm; sets reasonable limits and follows through when the child tests limits; encourages independence, yet is available when the child needs to be dependent; respects the child's space; and takes care of booboos. This is what a play therapist is: The Good Mother.

Homework

You should have completed the five simulated sessions with your adult partner by now. It is time to begin practicing with a child. The purpose of this practice is to provide you with the opportunity to use your microskills and observe how the child responds in the play situation. The child should not be a real client who was referred for counseling. Instead, recruit the child of a friend or relative, or use one of your own children. The age of the child should be between four and nine years of age, and be sure to choose a child who you are confident does not have any serious emotional problems. You are to spend six to eight 30-minute practice sessions with this child. This should allow you time to not only practice skills, but to also observe the play therapy process. After every two to three sessions, complete one of the self-evaluations provided on the following pages.

Play Session Self Assessment

1. With which toys did you feel most comfortable? Why?

2. With which toys did you feel most uncomfortable? Why?

3. Did you experience any particular thoughts in relation to certain play activities (memories, visualizations, etc.)?
   Play Activity   Thought

4. Did you experience any strong feelings in relation to certain play activities?
   Play Activity   Feeling

5. What limitsetting situations occurred, and how did you respond to them?

6. List any questions you have about play therapy at this point.
   Limitsetting Situation   Response

7. Rate your comfort level with play therapy.

   | 1 | 2 | 3 | 4 | 5 | 6 | 7 |

   Very Uncomfortable   Very Comfortable

PLAY SESSION SELF ASSESSMENT

1. With which toys did you feel most comfortable? Why?

2. With which toys did you feel most uncomfortable? Why?

3. Did you experience any particular thoughts in relation to certain play activities (memories, visualizations, etc.)?
   Play Activity   Thought

4. Did you experience any strong feelings in relation to certain play activities?
   Play Activity   Feeling

5. What limitsetting situations occurred, and how did you respond to them?

6. List any questions you have about play therapy at this point.
   Limitsetting Situation   Response

7. Rate your comfort level with play therapy.

   　　　1　　2　　3　　4　　5　　6　　7
   Very Uncomfortable   Very Comfortable

PLAY SESSION SELF ASSESSMENT

1. With which toys did you feel most comfortable? Why?

2. With which toys did you feel most uncomfortable? Why?

3. Did you experience any particular thoughts in relation to certain play activities (memories, visualizations, etc.)?
   Play Activity   Thought

4. Did you experience any strong feelings in relation to certain play activities?
   Play Activity   Feeling

5. What limitsetting situations occurred, and how did you respond to them?

6. List any questions you have about play therapy at this point.
   Limitsetting Situation   Response

7. Rate your comfort level with play therapy.

       1   2   3   4   5   6   7
   Very Uncomfortable   Very Comfortable

CHAPTER 8

Therapeutic Process

Why talk about process? Understanding the process that occurs in play therapy or any type of counseling is necessary in order to understand what types of phenomena and behavior are normal and expectable, and what types are not. The former provides common benchmarks for gauging therapeutic progress, while the latter provides insight into the unique issues of a particular child. Thus, knowledge of typical process phenomena provides an important conceptual template to the counselor. The purpose of this chapter is to review some of the theoretical models and research findings regarding therapeutic process in order to help you start building your own template of the play therapy process.

A General Process Model

Counseling, and psychotherapy in general, is a process which progresses through stages. Depending on the frame of reference – that is your theoretical foundation and research background – conceptualizations of counseling process range from three to nine stages or more (Carkhuff & Berenson, 1977; Egan, 1994). It is clear that there are distinct behaviors that occur in the first therapy session that are different from behaviors in the last therapy session in a successful counseling relationship. For the sake of simplicity, I will begin with a discussion of Carkhuff's and Berenson's description of the counseling process with adult clients.

Carkhuff and Berenson identified three stages: exploration, understanding, and action (Figure 8-1, following page). The first stage, or downward phase, is characterized by development of the therapeutic alliance and clients "telling their stories." At the beginning of the stage, clients tend to be vague and general, with the counselor's job being to clarify and help the client become more specific and focused. As this occurs, the client develops a clearer understanding of issues, conflicts, feelings, behaviors, and thoughts, and the connections among them. At this point, the client has entered the stage of understanding or the bottom phase of counseling. Once clients develop clear understanding of issues, they can then move on to think about options for dealing with the issues. By the end of this stage, the client has narrowed down these options and is focusing on specific courses of action. The counseling process then progresses to the action stage or upward phase. This stage is characterized by the client choosing and implementing options in order to effect change. Carkhuff and Berenson did not think of counseling as a seamless process that moves sequentially from one stage to the next. They see this more as a series of mini-processes in which the client moves from exploring to understanding to action regarding one problem, which in turn leads to exploring, understanding, and action in a related area, and so forth.

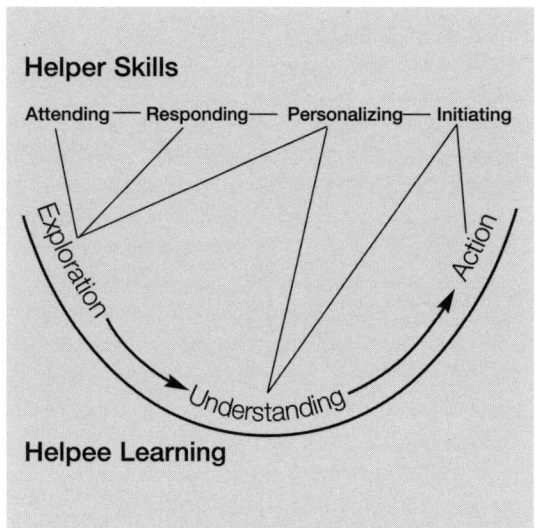

FIGURE 8-1 HELPING PROCESS – CARKHUFF & BERENSON MODEL (1977)

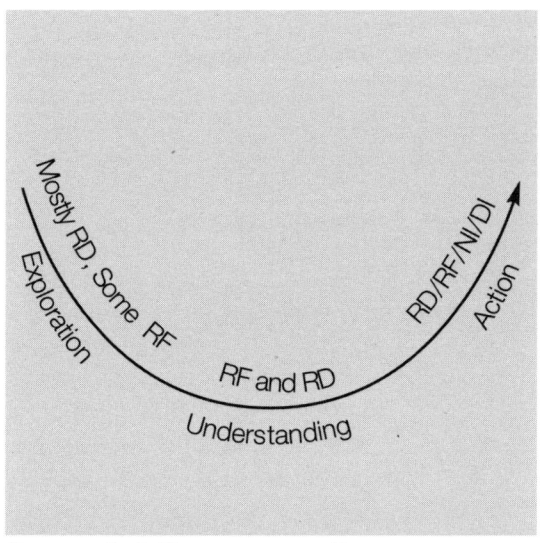

FIGURE 8-2 FACILITATIVE RESPONSES IN THE PLAY THERAPY

A simple extrapolation of this model to children does not require any quantum leap in thinking (Figure 8-2, at right). Early in the play therapy process, children play in an exploratory manner, trying out various toys and moving from theme to theme before they settle on more focused play with consistent themes. During this time, the counselor is using primarily reflective-descriptive responses and gradually moving to reflective-feeling responses. As the child's play becomes more focused, the counselor's responses become more specific, characterized by more reflective-feeling responses. The child has entered the stage of understanding and is moving toward action.

The term "action" applied to children differs somewhat from the definition used with adults. Some children who have entered the action stage may be simply working on issues in their play through repetition compulsion: that is, the recurring rituals and themes of their play. This would be more commonly observed with such problems as trauma related to disasters or child abuse. "Action," here, really refers to working through internal issues. In these cases the counselor will continue using descriptive and feeling responses, and move in the direction of helping the child utilize the metaphor. The counselor might also use non-directive and directive intervention responses, but to a lesser extent than the reflective responses.

EXAMPLE

A seven-year-old girl who was sexually abused replays this scenario over several sessions. She makes snakes out of Play-Doh and has them surround and attack mother and baby family figures.

Counselor:	The snakes are hurting the mommy and baby again. (RD)
Client:	*They're going to kill them.*
Counselor:	Who's going to kill?
Client:	*The snakes. The snakes are going to kill the mommy and baby.*
Counselor:	The mommy and baby feel pretty helpless. (RF)
Client:	*They can't do nothing.*
Counselor:	The mommy and baby are always getting hurt by the snakes. (RD)
Client:	*Yes.*
Counselor:	I wonder if there's something the mommy and baby could do to protect themselves? (NI)
Client:	*I don't know.*
Counselor:	If the mommy and baby protected themselves would they run away, or fight the snakes, or get someone to help them? (DI) Etc.

Other children in this stage will be focusing on more concrete action. For instance, an anxious child might benefit from learning simple relaxation techniques. This will require that the counselor teach the child a skill, and that the child practice the skill outside of the counseling session. In this situation, the counselor is using intervention responses almost exclusively. The counselor is meeting the child's needs through direct intervention.

EXAMPLE

Seven year old boy who has expressed general anxiety in his play.

(Counselor speaking) We're going to do something a little different today. Remember last time when you said you would like to not worry? Well I'm going to teach you a trick that will help you relax and worry less. We will do this for about ten minutes today, and then you may begin playing. First, I want you to get as comfortable as you can in your chair.

Etc. (This training is a directive intervention type communication.)

PLAY THERAPY PROCESS MODELS

There are a few models of play therapy process that have been proposed over the years. These models are based on either clinical observations or observational research. Two of these models are discussed below.

Nordling and Guerney (1999) have proposed a very practical conceptual framework for the Child-Centered play therapy process based on common observable play behaviors. They have delineated four stages in play therapy: warm-up, aggressive, regressive, and mastery stages. During the warm-up stage, children familiarize themselves with the playroom structure and toys, and develop a sense of trust in the therapist. Experimentation with the playroom environment and the therapist occurs during this stage. This may vary from low level limit testing by oppositional children to inhibited behavior by anxious and withdrawn children. The therapist's task during this stage is to convey PEGS consistently, establishing an accepting, empathetic, and permissive relationship with the child.

Once children have developed trust for and comfort with the therapist, the real therapeutic work begins. Nordling and Guerney believe that the first therapeutic issue is the need to express emotions, the primary themes being anger and control. They see this occurring in generalized aggressive play, such as hitting the bobo doll, making messes, and pretend aggressive scenarios involving the therapist. As children work through this stage they begin to gain a sense of self-control and have practiced more adaptive interpersonal behaviors. From this stage, the client progresses to the regressive stage.

In the regressive stage, the themes of children's play shifts to issues related to attachment, nurturance, and the interplay of dependence-independence needs. What allows this to happen is the deepened sense of trust and self-control which has developed during the aggressive stage. Thus, the child can now feel comfortable to display behaviors characteristic of younger children, such as baby talk, nursing from a bottle, or being "tucked in" for a nap. The child may also engage in caregiving behaviors, pretending to be a parent who is caring for a doll or the therapist. These behaviors begin to dissipate as the child works through these issues.

The final stage of the play therapy process according to Nordling and Guerney, is the mastery stage. This stage is characterized by assertive, self-directed play in which the child takes the initiative to complete building or art projects, create and play games, and overcome obstacles that occur in play. These obstacles may be real, such as having to create or transform an object for use in the play, or part of a pretend in which the child portrays herself as overcoming an obstacle. As children complete their therapeutic work, the play typically shifts from specific themes to less focused play, such as board games or general art projects and the like. The child has done the work he needs to do and has, in effect, run out of gas.

Jernberg (1979) described a somewhat similar process in her play therapy approach, Theraplay, a developmentally-based directive type of play therapy. In Theraplay, the therapist prescribes play activities for the child based on perceived developmental needs. Jernberg outlined five stages that were identified through observational research on this approach: exploration, tentative acceptance, negative reaction, growing and trusting, and termination. In the exploration stage, the child develops a sense of the therapist, an understanding of the structure of the therapy session, and the idea that fun is part of the therapy. This moves into the tentative acceptance stage, during which the child appears to be "playing the therapy game" but has not really committed to the therapy or the therapist. This stage is characterized by what seem to be overreactions of the child to the play activities and checking for therapist reactions to the child's play. Jernberg sees this as an indicator that the child has not yet developed trust in the therapist. The negative reaction stage is characterized by resistance to the therapy and rejection of the therapist. During this stage, it is not unusual for children to test limits, refuse to participate, attempt to leave the playroom, and tantrum. If the therapist remains consistent and firm regarding the direction of the therapy, the child eventually commits and becomes genuinely involved in the play activities. Jernberg views this as a sign that the child trusts the therapist and is willing to collaborate in the therapy.

The growing and trusting stage is where much of the working through occurs in the Theraplay process. During this stage, the child actively and willingly engages in the activities prescribed by the therapist to address the child's developmental needs. The therapist may also invite the child's parents to become involved in the therapy, coaching them on their participation with the child. Through observations of the child's behavior and parent-child interactions, the therapist determines that the child's issues and needs have been addressed, moving the child into the termination stage. Jernberg conceives of termination as a process that incorporates three substages: announcement, planning, and the final session. During this stage, the child's growth, strengths, and positive changes are emphasized, and the child is moved back into everyday activities as quickly as possible.

I have developed my own conceptualization of the play therapy process, which I see mirroring the developmental stages proposed by Erikson (1963). I base my ideas on the observation that the therapeutic relationship is very similar to the caregiver-child relationship. Thus, the child must accomplish tasks in play therapy which are similar to the developmental tasks of Erikson's early and middle childhood psychosocial stages.

The first stage of Erikson's model is the Basic Trust vs. Mistrust (birth to age 2) psychosocial crisis. This stage involves the development of the understanding that one's basic needs for food, warmth, shelter, nurturance, etc., will be met. The basic trust to which Erikson refers is trust in one's caregivers – that they will predictably meet these needs. The early stage of play therapy parallels this developmental stage in the development of the counselor-client relationship. Just as the infant must develop basic trust, the client must develop an understanding of the counselor as a predictable person who will meet the child's therapeutic needs. These include helping the child understand the structure of therapy and limits, as well as establishing the necessary therapeutic conditions (Rogers, 1959).

Erikson labeled the second psychosocial crisis Autonomy vs. Shame and Doubt (ages 2-3). In this stage, the child's primary developmental task is to establish a sense of self separate from the primary caregiver, yet still connected. During this stage, the child is able to move away from the caregiver as a result of better locomotion skills and interaction with peers. The child also exerts his independence by controlling eating and toileting, as he develops the muscular control necessary for toilet training. This helps the child develop a sense of independence. Again, I see a parallel between this developmental stage and the second stage of play therapy. After the child has developed a sense of trust in the play therapist and the predictability of the play therapy situation, the child is then free to begin generating her own play without having to look to the counselor for approval. The child can experiment with exerting control, metaphorically through pretends, directly through limit testing, or by "ordering" the counselor to do things. The counselor's task is to encourage the child to be self-directed, while being consistent in maintaining the rules and structure of the playroom.

The primary psychosocial crisis in Erikson's third stage is Initiative vs. Guilt. During this stage, the child experiences curiosity about her world and begins to explore and experiment to discover her capabilities and how these affect the individuals around her. The caregiver's task is to encourage this curiosity and initiative taking – to communicate that it is desirable to be curious. Similarly in play therapy, the child progresses to an initiative taking stage in which the play becomes more child-directed and focused. The child initiates play activities spontaneously, develops pretends without seeking the counselor's help, and directs the counselor's involvement. This allows the child to utilize the play to work through issues in the next stage.

Erikson labeled the psychosocial crisis that spans most of middle childhood as Industry vs. Inferiority. He proposed that the primary task of this stage is to develop a sense of oneself as a productive individual within the context of one's primary social environment. In Western culture, this involves productivity in school. However, if a child is not a successful student, then, in order to successfully resolve this developmental crisis, he needs to find other avenues for being productive, such as athletics or hobbies. The Industry that occurs in play therapy is related to the use of the play to work through issues, conflicts, and feelings. During this stage, the repetitive metaphors and rituals that are characteristic of the repetition compulsion are more evident. This is also the stage during which therapist directed interventions may be introduced, such as skill training and modeling, by mutual agreement with the child. This is the working stage of therapy, similar to Jernberg's (1979) "Growing and Trusting" stage, and Carkhuff and Berenson's (1977) "Action" stage.

I see the termination stage of play therapy as mirroring Erikson's adolescent psychosocial crisis of Identity vs. Identity Diffusion. Erikson sees adolescence as a time during which individuals must establish a sense of self that is independent of their families, yet still connected by the usual family ties. This sets the stage for functioning as an independent adult who has a sense of continuity with the past. When the child has finished the work of play therapy, he, in effect, has developed a sense of independence from the counselor. The child has resolved issues and developed skills that allow him to be emotionally self-supporting. He no longer needs the counselor. At the same time, the child has a sense that the counselor will be there for him if the child needs help in the future. This harkens back to the idea discussed in chapter five of the counselor as "good mother."

Research on Play Therapy Process

Research on play therapy process, though sparse, does lend support to these conceptualizations. Observational research by Hendricks (1971, in Landreth, 1991) of behaviors over 24 sessions of play therapy revealed some distinct patterns that were evident in the play therapy process. During the first four sessions, play tended to be exploratory and tentative, with negative emotions less likely to be expressed. From the fifth through the eighth sessions, general aggressive play and some limit testing were observed. During the ninth through twelfth sessions, aggressive play became more specific and theme oriented, more negative feelings were expressed, and clients were checking with the therapist for signs of disapproval. This type of play continued through the twentieth session, with the addition of increased disclosure by clients about their families, and more initiation of interactive play with the therapist. As the process concluded in sessions 21 through 24, clients began expressing positive feelings, initiating pretends, and finally became less focused as issues appeared to be resolved.

Research conducted by Sloan (1997) also revealed a pattern to aggressive play over ten sessions of play therapy. Sloan's observers reported an increase in aggressive play (including verbal aggression) between the fourth and seventh sessions of therapy. Aggressive play decreased after the seventh session.

Summary

When all of this information is distilled down, what we end up with is a relatively simple process that consists of four stages. First, there is a stage in which the child learns to trust the counselor and the relationship develops. Next, you can expect a period of some resistance, which is evident in some aggressive behavior and limit testing. Third, there is a working stage during which clients feel comfortable enough to express themselves openly and free to initiate play, converse, and self-disclose. Finally, there is a termination stage in which the child and therapist must disengage with each other in a healthy way.

What you have to keep in mind after reading this chapter is that the conceptualizations of therapeutic process presented above are constructions. They are labels placed on sets of consistent behaviors that have been observed by the "experts" who developed these models. They are not absolute fact, do not occur with every client, and are not truth. These models have been developed simply as guideposts for practitioners to understand what they might be experiencing in play therapy. In effect, they are the developer's personal theory of counseling (or, as I call mine, my psychotic fantasy of counseling). Thus, they have some general explanatory value, but must be applied with caution to specific clients. Because of the uniqueness of individuals, you must be prepared to create a new theory of counseling for every client who walks in the door. These models provide some tools from which to synthesize your own theory of counseling process.

Homework

At this point in your do-it-yourself training, you should be working with a practice child "client." Using the conceptualizations of therapy process presented, describe the therapeutic process to date, and behaviors that support your conceptualization. Since this should not be a real client, do not focus on perceived therapeutic issues. Simply think about process. You should continue meeting with this child for the eight sessions recommended in the previous chapter.

Nordling & Guerney

Stage: _____

Behaviors: _____

_____

_____

Jernberg

Stage: _____

Behaviors: _____

_____

_____

Cerio

Stage: _____

Behaviors: _____

_____

_____

CHAPTER 9

Transference and Countertransference

Transference and countertransference are old psychoanalytic terms that are bandied about quite a bit by clinicians. These constructs focus on certain types of interactions that occur between therapist and client which either facilitate or impede the therapeutic process. While the psychoanalytic ideas regarding these phenomena connect them with specific issues related to specific periods of development (Arlow, 1989), the discussion here will utilize these terms more generically to describe therapeutic phenomena. The purpose of this chapter is to provide the reader with a brief overview of issues that arise out of the counselor-client relationship, and to provide ideas regarding how to address these issues when they interfere with the counseling process.

WHAT IS TRANSFERENCE?

Transference in the most general sense occurs when a client brings issues, emotions, and conflicts from outside the therapy room and projects (or transfers) them onto the counselor. It is a process that flows from client to counselor. Although these issues may have nothing to do with the counselor, the client behaves *as if* they do. For example, an adult client I was seeing had a difficult time finding a parking place before her session. When she entered the therapy room, she immediately began yelling at me about her parking problem, transferring the frustration she was feeling by directing it at me. In its simplest sense, transference can be defined as having a difficult day at work, then going home and kicking the dog.

Transference is one of the basic elements of traditional psychoanalysis. In this approach therapists present themselves as "blank slates" in order to serve as templates for client transference (Arlow). As transference occurs, the therapist analyzes the meaning of the transferred material in terms of unresolved psychological conflicts of early childhood. As the client develops insight into the meaning of recurring transference, he gradually resolves the conflict, reducing anxiety and the use of defense mechanisms.

The Person-Centered approach, on which more child-centered play therapy approaches are based, does not recognize the idea of transference as a useful component of counseling and therapy. Rogers, in fact, considered the conceptualization of client feelings and reaction in terms of transference to be disrespectful of the client's experience (Rogers, 1965). Thus, instead of interpreting client reactions as related to past experience, Rogers focused on the here-and-now interactions between client and therapist and how these affected the client.

The definition of transference I proposed above takes a middle position between these two theoretical schemas for practical reasons. In child therapy, there is a power differential between counselor and child that is much more profound than the one that exists between adult clients and therapists. This power differential exists because children function in a world controlled by adults. When a child enters into a counseling relationship with an adult, the child's frame of reference is based on the child's experience with other adult-child relationships. Thus, the child relates to the counselor based on what the child knows: parent-child, teacher-child, and principal-child interactions, for example. The manner in which the child relates is a form of transference – parent/adult authority figure transference. Denying that this type of transference exists in play therapy would be disrespectful of the child's experience. The manner in which counselors deal with this transference is another matter.

My approach to transference is practical and independent of allegiances to any particular models. I believe that transference needs to be viewed as a reflection of the child's experience and used as a constructive element of therapy. The transference that occurs tells me much about the child's perceptions of adults and the conflicts that the child may be rehashing. Transference is an integral part of the working through process.

Types of Transference

O'Connor (1991) described three types of transference that commonly occur in play therapy: parental, all powerful therapist, and disengagement difficulties. Parental transference, as alluded to above, is the most common type that occurs in play therapy. In school settings, the definition of this can be expanded to include most of the adult authority figures with whom children have contact. Signs of this type of transference are listed at right.

1. Client calls the counselor mom or dad, irrespective of gender (O'Connor).
2. Client engages the counselor in such activities as regressive nurturing type play (nursing from a bottle, rocking in a cradle).
3. Client asks the counselor about the counselor's experience as a parent.
4. Client idealizes the counselor as a parent.
5. Client tests limits with counselor as the client does with a parent or teacher.
6. Client acts out issues with the counselor that the client has with a parent or teacher.
7. Client talks to his or her parents about the virtues of the counselor versus the client's perceptions of the parents' deficits.

Transference involving perception of the therapist as all powerful is often characterized by one or more of the following:

1. Client looks to the counselor to solve the client's problems for him or her.
2. Client idealizes the counselor as a person, that is, puts the counselor "on a pedestal."
3. Client becomes upset when the counselor is unable or unwilling to help in a particular situation.

The third type of transference, difficulty disengaging, occurs when the client takes the content of the therapy outside of the playroom. Some signs that this is occurring include:

1. Client leaves the therapy room upset or overstimulated, and acts out in the classroom or at home.
2. Client continues a play behavior in the classroom or at home, such as baby talk or a fantasy.
3. Client talks about an issue that was stimulated in the therapy at an inappropriate time, such as a classroom discussion.

Transference is not automatically bad or good in terms of the effect on the therapeutic process. I find it useful to think of situations in terms of constructive or positive transference, and unconstructive or negative transference. Positive transference adds to the therapy by serving as a vehicle for clients to work through issues and conflicts they have with adults.

EXAMPLE
A boy who has been physically abused by his father, pretends to call the police and have the male counselor arrested and put in jail because the counselor is "bad."

On the other hand, there are times when transference becomes an inhibiting factor in the therapy. This negative transference interferes with the therapy process by presenting roadblocks to progress, such as overdependence on or idealization of the therapist, parental or teacher resentment, and boundary problems outside of the playroom.

EXAMPLE
A nine-year-old third grade female spends her session playing with the dollhouse, rearranging the furniture and burying the baby doll in the sandbox. During the session, she verbalizes that she feels that her mother doesn't like her. Later that day, during a classroom discussion about things that make people happy, the girl reveals the following: She's happy because her mother had thought about having an abortion when she was pregnant with the girl but decided not to.

This is a real situation that occurred when I was working in a school setting. The girl's play had stimulated the feelings of rejection the girl experienced from her mother. The memory of her mother's story either was not recalled or not disclosed during the play session. Instead, the child took the content of the session back to class with her, and inappropriately disclosed this information to the entire class, including me and the teacher. This created some problems for the girl with the other students, and for the teacher and me in relation to parent inquiries about this discussion.

Considering O'Connor's classifications described above, I like to further delineate transference into positive and negative categories.

Positive Transference:
1. Client calls the counselor mom or dad, irrespective of gender (O'Connor).
2. Client engages the counselor in such activities as regressive nurturing type play (nursing from a bottle, rocking in a cradle).
3. Client calls the counselor "teacher" or "principal."
4. Client acts out classroom or home situations with the counselor.
5. Client tests limits with counselor as the client does with a parent or teacher.

Negative Transference:
1. Client asks the counselor about the counselor's experience as a parent.
2. Client idealizes the counselor as a parent.
3. Client talks to his or her parents about the virtues of the counselor versus the client's perceptions of the parents' deficits.
4. Client looks to the counselor to solve the client's problems for him or her.
5. Client idealizes the counselor as a person, that is, puts the counselor "on a pedestal."
6. Client becomes upset when the counselor is unable or unwilling to help in a particular situation.
7. Client leaves the therapy room upset or overstimulated, and acts out in the classroom or at home.
8. Client continues a play behavior in the classroom or at home, such as baby talk or a fantasy.
9. Client talks about an issue that was stimulated in the therapy at an inappropriate time, such as a classroom discussion.

DEALING WITH TRANSFERENCE

In the case of positive transference, the way to respond is to "go with the flow" and allow the child to discharge feelings and work through issues. The counselor will be using mostly reflective-descriptive and reflective-feeling responses in these transference situations, which convey respect for the child's experience without interpreting (and, therefore, interrupting) the transference. Thus, in cases in which the child is primarily projecting issues in a non-threatening manner, responding within the transference can be very productive to the therapeutic work.

Take again the example of the little boy who was punishing the counselor, described above. A child-centered therapist would look at this as a simple expression of the child's anger at the counselor or anxiety about the counseling situation. However, this type of play provides a metaphor of the child's family experience: The counselor is a bad male who needs to be punished, just as the boy's father was punished for the abuse he inflicted. Transference allowed the boy to act out these feelings by projecting them onto the counselor, a safe individual who is not going to harm the child. While the conceptualization of traditional child-centered approaches disregards transference, the manner in which child-centered therapists would respond to the child in this example would be consistent with the methods described above. That is, the therapist would allow the child to develop this metaphor by reflecting and summarizing, without interpreting the possible meaning of the play.

EXAMPLE
A boy who has been physically abused by his father, pretends to call the police and have the male counselor arrested and put in jail because the counselor is "bad."

Client: *You've been bad. I have to call the police and have you put in jail.*
Counselor: You want me to go to jail because I've been bad.
Client: *Ya, you go to jail.*
Counselor: I have to go to jail now.
Client: *You go to jail over there (indicates corner). You're bad.*
Counselor: I must have done something very bad for you to want me to go to jail. Etc.

Responding to negative transference requires slightly different approaches, depending on the type of negative transference that is occurring. Let's look at some of these approaches.

REALITY TESTING

In cases in which the client idealizes the counselor, either as a parent, teacher, or "hero," it is important to do reality testing with the client. That is, the counselor needs to help the child realize that the counselor is human and fallible *without* diminishing the child's frame of reference, as much as possible.

EXAMPLE
Client: *You know, I wish my father was like you. You wouldn't hurt your kids like that.*
Counselor: You like to think of me as not being hard.
Client: *Yea. I know you wouldn't be mean to kids.*
Counselor: I know in here, I try to be as helpful to you as I can be. But I have to tell you that when I am a parent, I have to be strict sometimes. I am different when I am a parent.

Client: Yea, but I bet you don't hurt your kids feelings.
Counselor: The truth – sometimes I do. Being a counselor is different than being a parent. But I know you appreciate the way I am when I am with you. That's what's special about our time together.
Client: Yea, but I still know you wouldn't be mean.
Counselor: Well, it's important for you to think about me in this way RIGHT NOW.

In this example, the counselor validates the client's experience with the counselor first. Then, the counselor provides the client with factual information in order to modify the client's idealization to help the client differentiate the counselor-client interaction from the parent-child interaction. The counselor does this respectfully and does not try to force the child to change his perception. When the child continues to be insistent at the end of this segment, by saying, "right now," the counselor accepts the child's need to see the counselor this way, but qualifies this perception as a "here-and-now" experience. This leaves open the possibility that this perception can change in the future.

The first example focused on a form of parental idealization that is unconstructive. Let's look at a different type of idealization.

EXAMPLE
Client: My teacher took recess away.
Counselor: So you're upset.
Client: Yea, it isn't fair. She said I was bothering other students.
Counselor: Were you?
Client: I got up to sharpen my pencil. Then Justin called me a name, so I took his pencil. Would you talk to my teacher and see if she'll let me go outside. I'll be good the rest of the day.
Counselor: So, you were bothering Justin.
Client: But he started it. It isn't fair.
Counselor: I would probably feel the same way if I were you.
Client: Will you talk to her?
Counselor: You chose to be out of your seat, and the teacher has consequences for that.
Client: But it isn't fair.
Counselor: I know that you feel that the teacher isn't being fair. But she has her consequences, and I can't change those once you have chosen to break her rules.
Client: But you said you would help me.
Counselor: I can help you work on making better choices, or work out a contract with the teacher. But I can't change the consequences once you have made a choice.

In this negative transference situation, the counselor again respects the child's perception that things aren't fair. However, the counselor does not buy into the child's request that the counselor fix things. The counselor places responsibility back on the child and reality tests by clarifying what the counselor's role is in relation to the teacher-student interaction.

TRANSITION RITUALS

Transition rituals are useful in negative transference situations in which the client leaves the playroom upset or overstimulated, continues play behavior in class or at home, or discusses therapy issues at inappropriate times or in inappropriate places. These situations indicate that the child has difficulties delineating the boundaries between the counseling situation and everyday life. That is, the client doesn't understand where and when the rules for behavior in counseling stop and the rules for behavior outside of counseling begin. A transition ritual is a way of creating a boundary by having a period of time that is neither counseling nor everyday life, in which the child adjusts to the move back to the classroom or home. It is more or less a planned time-out.

The type of transition ritual that is used depends on the type of transition problem a client is exhibiting. For children who become overstimulated or have difficulty discontinuing with play, it helps to plan a quiet time of about five minutes at the end of each session. This can include any of the following:

1. Lights out and head down to rest.
2. A metaphorical story involving self-control and calmness.
3. Reading one chapter per session from a book that interests the child, so the child will look forward to the transition time.
4. An ongoing story told by the counselor, similar to the chapter book activity.
5. A formal progressive relaxation.

For children who bring up counseling issues inappropriately, usually direct reminders about the differences between the in-therapy and out-of-therapy environments is useful. Some examples are provided below.

- Remember, the rules in here are different than the rules in your class. When you are in class, you are expected to follow your teacher's rules.
- In here it's okay to pretend, but time's up now. When you go back to the room, pretending is done and it's time to work.
- When I open the door to your room, you need to walk quietly to your seat, take out your book, and join the class.
- There are some things that are okay to say in my office that you are not allowed to say outside of my office. If you choose to say them and I overhear you, you are choosing to have me enforce the school rules.

With some children, particularly younger children who are more concrete in their thinking, combining concrete reinforcers with reminders is sometimes necessary. This involves selecting reinforcers that the client values, establishing the reinforcement contingency with the child, and then reminding the child about both the expected behavior and the contingency. Token reinforcers (poker chips, stickers, cotton balls) can be useful in this respect, a certain amount of which the child must earn in order to receive a reward. Very young children sometimes require immediate reinforcement, such as candy, stickers, and pencils, until they are able to consistently behave appropriately.

ORIENTATION ACTIVITIES

A third method for dealing with negative transference is by providing an orientation to counseling for the adults who have contact with the child (parents, teachers, administrators). The goal of this method is to help adults understand the therapy approach and process, and to prepare them for certain behaviors that clients may exhibit in reaction to the therapy. General orientations, such as group presentations are helpful in introducing parents and teachers to play therapy. A guide for presenting this type of orientation is provided in Chapter 12. Individual orientation of parents and teachers is also useful following referral of children for counseling. This provides the parents with some ideas of what to expect based on the specific problem for which a child is referred.

One piece of information that I have found especially helpful to both parents and teachers is a description of the therapeutic process. Typically adults expect children to be happy and problem-free at the end of every counseling session. Thus, when a child begins to touch on unpleasant issues and leaves a session upset, the adults become frustrated and conclude that the therapy is not working. Consequently, it is important to provide the adults with a realistic description of the therapeutic process in order to help them understand what is going on with their child. I describe therapy as a journey of gradual change that involves peaks and valleys along the way. There are times when children leave sessions happy and content, but there are also times when they are upset because the therapy has stimulated unpleasant feelings and thoughts. When this occurs, children will sometimes exhibit their upset in class or at home. Rather than indicating that counseling is not working, this is a sign that the child is making progress, but will need time to work through the issue that is causing the upset.

In addition to providing orientation activities, it is important for counselors to encourage adults to maintain contact with the counselors. Again with individual parents and teachers, I ask them to contact me if a child is particularly upset, or the child's behavior becomes problematic after a counseling session. With children I saw regularly in a school setting, I sent a standard letter to parents once per month, reminding them that their child was receiving counseling from me, and encouraging them to contact me if they had any questions or concerns. It is important for counselors to keep in mind that children do not function in a vacuum, and that the primary adults in a child's life significantly impact the child's functioning. Orientation activities and regular parent/teacher contacts are ways to involve significant adults in the therapeutic process.

COUNTERTRANSFERENCE: WHAT PUSHES YOUR BUTTONS?

Just as clients experience transference with the counselor, counselors also experience transference with clients. This *countertransference* is the counselor's reaction to the client as a result of feelings, issues, beliefs, and experiences that are not directly connected with the therapy (Watkins, 1985). That is, the counselor brings these issues into the therapy room and transfers or projects them onto the client. These are issues which humanistic approaches call blindspots or softspots (Egan, 1994). Before we explore this phenomenon, it is important to think about your own softspots. Complete the activity on the next two pages, and then continue on with the chapter.

What Pushes Your Buttons?

Directions: Complete the sentence stems below. When you are finished, reread your responses and rank order the five statements to which you have the strongest emotional response.

1. My biggest problem is _____

2. The most frequent negative feelings in my life are _____

3. These feelings occur when _____

4. Some things that adults do that are hurtful to kids are _____

5. Some things that kids do, that are hurtful to kids are _____

6. The social setting I find most troublesome is _____

7. The person I have most trouble with is _____

8. Life would be better if _____

9. I don't cope very well with _____

10. I get anxious when _____

11. What others like most about me is _____
_____

12. What others dislike most about me is _____
_____

13. If I could change one thing about myself it would be _____
_____

14. A very unpleasant childhood experience I remember is _____
_____

15. A very pleasant childhood experience I recall is _____
_____

16. I lack confidence about _____
_____

17. I feel competent about _____
_____

18. I still haven't got over _____
_____

19. Something that really pushes my buttons is _____
_____

20. I would like to improve _____
_____

Is countertransference always bad? That is, when a counselor experiences countertransference toward a particular client, does it always interfere with the therapy process? My answer to this is no, because in the broadest sense, deep empathy for a client can be thought of as a form of positive countertransference. When a counselor develops a relationship with a client, particularly a child, this usually involves some feelings of caring, concern, and protectiveness. These feelings are necessary for understanding the child's world. However, if the counselor begins to overidentify with the client – that is, cross the boundary between self and other – then the relationship can actually be detrimental to the client (Rogers, 1975), and the countertransference is a negative factor in the therapy. This is the type of countertransference about which you need to be concerned as a play therapist, and the type on which this chapter will focus.

Types of Countertransference

Just as was true with transference, there are several types of countertransference that are common to child therapy (O'Connor, 1991). The discussion here will focus on four common types: parental, authority figure, overidentification, and challenges to therapist competence.

Parental Countertransference

Parental countertransference is the therapist's tendency to respond to the client as a parent would when it is not appropriate to do so. It is commonly manifested in such therapist behaviors as unnecessary limitsetting, directing and advising of the child; overidentification with the child's parents and representing their viewpoint; and inappropriate caretaking of the child (that is, doing something for the child which the child is capable of doing). Parental countertransference is a product of blindspots and softspots related to counselors' experiences with their families of origin, and as parents themselves. The problem with this type of countertransference is that it interferes with counselors' capacities to understand children's frames of reference, and consequently, their experiences, feelings, and reactions. The counselor, in effect, becomes the parents' representative in the playroom.

EXAMPLE
A counselor finds himself becoming aggravated by a client who consistently makes big messes in the playroom. The counselor is continually cleaning up after the child during sessions, and sometimes stops the child from doing something that is actually permissible in the playroom environment. At home, the counselor is constantly overwhelmed by the messiness of his children.

Authority Figure Countertransference

This type of countertransference involves the therapist's tendency to overidentify with or conform to the expectations of non-parent authority figures in the child's life. It is common in settings such as schools or agencies in which there are multiple adults who are invested in a child's problem. It may be seen in such counselor behaviors as explaining teachers', principals', and other adults' perspectives to the child and devaluing the client's perspective; refusing to listen to or outright denial of the client's viewpoint; feeling pressure to utilize techniques or produce outcomes that will please the adults at the expense of the child; and feeling pressure to solve a problem within an inappropriately short period of time. What happens in this type of countertransference situation is that counselors find themselves focusing on the adult or institutional needs over those of the child. The counselor gets trapped in the position of being the representative of the probation officer, teacher, child protective worker, etc., which makes it impossible for the client to trust the counselor. The end result is that a true trusting, empathic relationship cannot develop between therapist and child.

EXAMPLE
When a counselor goes to a client's classroom to escort the child to the playroom, the child's teacher emerges with the child and says, "Make sure you speak with Justin about his talking in class." The counselor feels compelled to follow the teacher's directive, rather than continuing with the normal flow of therapy, and begins questioning the child about his behavior. The child withdraws and refuses to respond.

OVERIDENTIFICATION WITH THE CLIENT

This third type of negative countertransference is typically a product of therapists' experiences as children with their families of origin. This is the type of blindspot in which the therapist crosses the interpersonal boundary between counselor and child, and takes the role of "counselor knows best." That is, the counselor may think that the counselor knows what's best for the child because the counselor sees the child as being exactly like she was as a child. This leads to such counselor behaviors as inappropriately advising the child or parents to do something that the therapist did as a child, blindly taking the child's side in disputes with adults, shielding the child from consequences, and sympathetically overreacting to conflicts or problems the child experiences. While the counselor has a relationship with the child, it is not a healthy one, as it is based on the counselor's and not the child's experience. The child, then, becomes the counselor's tool for correcting the counselor's childhood experiences, which interferes with the resolution of the child's problems. In addition, this situation hinders the counselor's capacity to work with significant adults in the child's life.

EXAMPLE
A counselor who had behavior problems as a teenager begins seeing a teen who has a history of petty theft and running away from home. The client, who is bright and personable, disclosed information about his troubled relationship with his parents and his difficulty controlling his impulses. The counselor finds the boy to be very likeable and identifies closely with the boy's issues. During the course of counseling, the boy runs away again, stealing a car in the process. After the boy is apprehended, a meeting is requested by the boy's probation officer, which will include the parents, and the counselor. In the meeting, the counselor finds himself advocating for the boy to be given another chance, despite a very problematic history which suggests that the boy is a danger to others and lacks remorse.

CHALLENGES TO COUNSELOR COMPETENCE

The fourth type of negative countertransference involves situations in which counselors experience feelings of incompetence or of being overwhelmed. These feelings in turn generate feelings of anxiety, helplessness, frustration, and defensiveness, to name a few, which are then acted out with the client or with other adults involved with the client. For example, a counselor experiencing this type of countertransference might construe a simple and appropriate question from a teacher as a challenge to the counselor's expertise. The counselor responds inappropriately by being angry and defensive, thus, hindering the potential for collaboration with the teacher.

There are a number of factors that stimulate this type of blindspot. Certainly the counselor's type and level of training, and prior experience are important to the development of therapeutic self-efficacy (Taggart & Cerio, 1999). There are general differences among mental health professionals in terms of areas emphasized and depth of training. For instance, masters of social work programs are typically two years in length, with half of the training being classroom-based and the other half, field-based. While M.S.W.'s receive training in therapy, the focus of these programs is systems and public policy (Gazda, Childers, & Brooks, 1987). Accredited master degree programs in counseling require a minimum of three semesters of coursework, a part-time practicum, and a full-time semester long internship. The focus of these programs is counseling skills (Gazda et al.). More important than this, in relation to play therapy, is the type of play therapy training that these professionals receive. Taggart and Cerio, in a study of practicing school psychologists, found that school psychologists who used play therapy and reported the highest levels of therapeutic self-efficacy were individuals who had received experientially-based training. Cerio, Taggart, and Costa (1999), in a study of school counseling training programs, found that only a small percentage of programs offered such training, and that most training consisted of general overviews of the play therapy field. Thus, it is likely that a majority of entry level professionals who are using play therapy have little training in the approach, and are more at risk for experiencing the type of counter-transference related to competence.

A second factor contributing to this type of blindspot involves the setting in which the counselor practices. Counselors who are working in settings in which they are dealing with large caseloads or productivity demands may feel pressure to provide a "quick fix." This can lead to impatience or frustration with children whose therapy is progressing more slowly. In addition, settings such as schools, in which counselors experience expectations from other professionals in terms of resolving problems in short periods of time, or of utilizing certain types of approaches, can also generate pressure and impatience within the counselor. Counselors in these situations may feel compelled to inappropriately push the process along or to bring up issues at the request of other professionals which may not be therapeutically useful. The counselor ends up meeting the needs of the setting instead of the needs of the client.

Client preference is a third factor that can stimulate this type of countertransference. It is not unusual for counselors to find themselves to be more skilled in dealing with certain types of problems or clients. Conversely, there are usually certain types of clients or problems with which counselors feel completely ineffective. This may result in a counselor spending more time and effort on the clients with whom he feels he can be effective and less time on (or even avoiding) clients with whom he feels ineffective.

Finally, counselors' personal issues, particularly their general levels of self esteem and self-efficacy impact the competence blindspot. Counselors who suffer from low self esteem may very quickly begin to experience feelings of incompetence when confronted with a challenging client, problem, or situation, even if they have the competence to deal with the challenge. Counselors who have low levels of self-efficacy may find themselves easily discouraged and unwilling to utilize certain techniques that they know. Counselors may also experience feelings of incompetence stimulated by counseling situations that remind them of unresolved issues related to their own lives (Reid, 1980).

EXAMPLE

A very skilled counselor is presented with a seven-year old female client who refuses to do anything in the playroom. During the first two sessions of treatment, the child just sits at a table, staring and scowling at the wall, and refusing to talk. The counselor waited patiently for half of the first session, but as time went on, she felt herself become more and more frustrated with the client's behavior. The counselor tried to entice the child with toys and games, and then began asking the child questions. The client still refused to respond. This went on for a second session. With the third session looming, the counselor found herself feeling frustrated and impatient, deciding that if the child did not "cooperate" this time, the counselor would take her back to her room after five minutes.

DEALING WITH COUNTERTRANSFERENCE

The fact of the matter is that we all have blindspots and softspots that arise as we work with clients. The reality of therapeutic work is that it forces us to be consciously aware of our internal experiences. Hence, when a button gets pushed, we know it! The other reality is that most countertransference situations are not highly significant. That is, they do not require any kind of major response by the counselor. Three standard approaches for dealing with blindspots are: awareness, supervision, and therapy. Each succeeding method is more intensive than the previous one and, therefore, used with more pervasively interfering countertransference.

Awareness. For most low level blindspots, simply being aware of the issue is enough to prevent it from interfering with therapy. Awareness activities such as the one in this chapter are designed to help therapists deal with low level countertransference. Once aware of these blindspots, therapists can consciously process their reactions and redirect their attention in therapy when one of these blindspots is stimulated.

EXAMPLE

A counselor found herself daydreaming about things she used to play with as a child, while observing clients in therapy. When this happened she would lose track of what clients were doing. Becoming aware of this, the counselor began to monitor herself and interrupt her daydreaming whenever it occurred.

Supervision. Supervision is an excellent activity for processing countertransference. In supervision, counselors can identify and process blindspots with the help of a neutral supervisor or peer (Holloway, 1995; Zins, Maher, Murphy, & Wess, 1988). Thus, when simply being aware of a blindspot is not enough to prevent interference with therapy, a counselor should seek supervision of the situation to work through the counselor's reaction. This type of supervision does not require a "supervisor" who is officially and hierarchically above the counselor. Peer supervision is also useful, and, in the case of most school-based counselors, probably one of the only supervision resources available to them. Although formal supervision is usually structured as a face-to-face encounter with the supervisor serving more as an advisor and mentor, peer supervision can be less formal and more collaborative. At minimum, peer supervision can consist of a phone call to a respected peer for advice or simply as a sounding board. Peer supervision can be more formal, such as regular peer supervision groups, which have been found to be successful in meeting supervision needs of mental health professionals (Zins et al.).

EXAMPLE

A counselor found himself becoming angry and frustrated with an interaction with a parent. The counselor had tried to be empathetic and engaging with the parent, but these attempts were not only rejected, the parent attacked the counselor's expertise and credentials. Since the counselor was the only counselor in the school, he had no one to turn to regarding his feelings. Consequently, he called up a trusted friend who was a counselor in a neighboring district and vented his feelings with her. After listening to him, the friend validated the counselor's feelings, but was also able to help him identify why the interaction with this particular parent had stimulated such a strong reaction.

Therapy. While supervision provides a means of working through more complicated forms of countertransference, supervision is not therapy (Holloway, 1995). For countertransference situations which seriously interfere with the therapeutic process, or which cause significant distress for the therapist, therapy is usually recommended.

EXAMPLE

A male counselor who was adopted as a child, by chance receives several referrals for little boys who were abandoned by their mothers. The counselor had been involved in therapy during his adolescence specifically to deal with his feelings of being rejected by his biological mother, and thought he had resolved these issues. As a young adult, he located his biological mother and developed an amicable relationship with her. However, as the counselor saw these new clients, he became increasingly angry and depressed about their situations. Although he regularly vented these feelings during supervision sessions and understood the relationship of his reaction to his own life circumstances, the feelings persisted and intensified. The counselor realized that his own issues of abandonment had been stimulated by his work with his young clients, and that supervision did not provide an adequate way to deal with these issues. Thus, he elected to enter therapy again, and requested that he not be assigned clients dealing with similar issues until he had worked through his countertransference.

One thing I know from 25 years of contact with school and mental health counseling professionals is that people in these fields avoid seeking counseling like the plague. In spite of their understanding of the benefits of counseling, counselors often view their own need for help as a failure or a sign of weakness. There also appears to be an underlying assumption in the field that mental health professionals need to serve as models of good mental health. This is a myth. Counselors are people. People have problems. And when these problems fall outside the realm of "healer, heal thyself," then counselors need to seek help from another counseling professional.

Summary

Transference and countertransference are virtually unavoidable when adult counselors work with child clients. Because of this, counselors have a responsibility to recognize when either phenomenon is occurring, evaluate whether it is negatively impacting the counseling process, and take appropriate action to deal with the situation. In particular, it is the duty of counselors to be self-aware; that is, to understand their own blindspots and softspots, and to respond to countertransference by taking the most effective corrective action.

Blindspots and Softspots

Directions: It is time to examine in more depth areas that may contribute to negative countertransference. You most likely have some blindspots and softspots – attitudes, uncomfortable feelings, unresolved issues- regarding yourself and children that may interfere with your effectiveness as a helper.

Go back and review your responses on the previous activity in this chapter and on the self-evaluations of your play therapy practice. If you have experience counseling or teaching children, think about issues that might have developed during your career. Then complete the items on the following page. Be thoughtful and honest. You probably will not have blindspots in all the areas listed – don't feel compelled to have a blindspot if one does not exist. Just be honest with yourself.

BLINDSPOTS AND SOFTSPOTS

Blindspots Related to Parent Position:

Blindspots Related to Authority Figure Position:

Blindspots Related to Competence:

Blindspots Related to Your Childhood:

Blindspots Related to Cultural Differences:

Other Blindspots:

Chapter 10

Integrating Interventions

One of the things with which beginning play therapists often struggle is whether or not to adhere to a strict non-directive, child-centered approach. This seems to be more problematic in school settings, where counselors function within a network of demands from teachers, administrators, and parents, and where large numbers of clients and the structure of the school day create time constraints. Child-centered play therapy takes time, and most teachers want a child who is exhibiting behavioral problems to be "fixed" yesterday. Thus, rigidly adhering to this type of non-directive approach is not going to be the best practice with all clients in this type of setting. This, then, requires that counselors broaden their perspectives and think more divergently, integrating other approaches with play therapy in order to meet the needs of the client and the demands of the setting.

Let's return to two of the assumptions I stated in the introduction. The first is that the client-counselor relationship is critical to success in therapy (Lambert & Bergin, 1994). Play therapy is a means of developing this relationship through child appropriate activities (Landreth, 1991). This contention is supported by a recent study on group play therapy (Kaplewicz, 1999). One of the findings of the study was that children involved in a 10-session non-directive play therapy group were significantly more engaged with the therapist in fewer sessions (5) than children who participated in a group in which they simply received attention from an adult. The children in the play therapy condition remained more engaged with the therapist throughout the remaining five sessions of the group. Thus, if nothing else, play therapy at least facilitated the development of the therapeutic relationship. Once this is established, any number of techniques can be incorporated into the therapy.

The second assumption is that play therapy is only *one* of *many* counseling approaches that are appropriate for children. There are all kinds of approaches and techniques that can be used separately and incorporated into or used in conjunction with play therapy. What you use should be determined by the problem, the client's needs, and the setting. If you think in this way, then many possibilities for integration exist. You just need to determine how you want to integrate other approaches into play therapy. The purpose of this chapter is to provide you with a few examples of integration. Most of these are techniques that are integrated during the action or upward phase of therapy. So, the assumption is that you have used a more non-directive approach to explore and understand the child's experience in relation to a problem when you decide to implement one of these interventions.

PLAY THERAPY AND A CONCURRENT BEHAVIORAL INTERVENTION

Children who are experiencing emotional problems in schools usually come to the attention of professionals because of behavior problems in the classroom. Because these problems disrupt the classroom environment, one of the demands of the school setting is that the child stop exhibiting such problems *as soon as possible*. Since play therapy is a longer term approach, it is simply not effective to just use this when timeliness is so important.

In these situations, I typically chose to use play therapy in conjunction with behavior management techniques. In effect, I was doing two types of therapy concurrently, the connection between the two being the therapeutic relationship. My rationale for this type of approach is that the behavior management program targeted the symptom behavior, while the play therapy targeted the issues that stimulated the symptoms. Implementing this approach involved structuring the play therapy sessions slightly differently than the standard structure described above.

At the outset of counseling, I usually stay with a straightforward non-directive play therapy approach in order to allow time for the relationship to develop. While this usually takes two to three sessions, some clients will require more time than this to feel comfortable and trust the counselor. During this time, I also consult with the classroom teacher to establish the target behaviors on which the behavior management program will focus. The teacher and I also discuss the most appropriate type of program, reinforcement schedule, and reinforcers. For me, the most reasonable type of behavior management program to use is a token economy program. I have found that this type of program is less intrusive for teachers because I take responsibility for monitoring progress and providing rewards. The teacher's responsibility is to provide the token when the desired behavior occurs, or at predetermined intervals in which the desired behavior occurs.

When I sense that the relationship has been established, I negotiate a behavior contract with the child. I reserve the first portion of a session (10 to 15 minutes) for this activity. In this conference I ask the child about his concerns, state the teacher's concerns, and then try to blend these together. The child has input on which target behavior(s) will be included in the contract (Figure 10-1). I then explain the reinforcement schedule, and obtain information from the child regarding reinforcers that are desirable. With younger children, I present the teacher's ideas regarding rewards, and simply get feedback from them regarding which ones are more desirable. The more desirable ones will have the greatest value in a token economy program. With older children, I have them modify the teacher's list, adding other reasonable reinforcers and deleting those that have no value to the child.

I finish by explaining the reinforcement procedure to the client and then having the client sign the contract, which the teacher and I also sign. In the token economy procedure I use, the children have contract booklets, or charts on their desks (Figures 10-2 and 10-3). At the end of each interval of time, the teacher provides a token if the desired behavior occurs within the interval. With children below second grade level (and older children who are relatively immature) immediate reinforcement is usually necessary at the beginning of the program. Then, intervals of short duration are used until the behavior occurs frequently enough to lengthen the interval. With older children, daily reinforcement checks are adequate. Tokens need to be more concrete with younger children, such as stickers, stars, cotton balls, and poker chips. With older children the tokens can simply be checks in the contract booklet.

Once the contract has been negotiated, the client continues the session in the standard play therapy format. Subsequent sessions will be structured in two segments. The first segment, usually 25-35 minutes in schools and 40-45 minutes in mental health agencies, is the play therapy session. The second segment is comprised of a contract check and reinforcement. I total the checks received by the client and record this on a master chart in the client's folder (Figure 10-4). The client is then shown the reinforcement menu (Figure 10-5) that lists the reinforcers that were selected by client and teacher. Each reinforcer has a specific token value, with the most desirable ones requiring the most tokens in order to be purchased. The client can choose to "buy" a reinforcer, or choose to save tokens for a reinforcer of higher value. This choice is very important, as it gives the client some control in the reinforcement situation. The session ends after the contract check.

My Contract

Name _____

Goal 1:

Goal 2:

Goal 3:

Client's signature _____

Teacher's Signature _____

Counselor's Signature _____

Date _____

FIGURE 10-1 – CONTRACT FORM

108 *Play Therapy:* A Do-It-Yourself Guide for Practitioners

My Contract

Name_____

Teacher_____

Month of_____

Goal #1

Goal #2

Goal #3

Fold 1

Fold 2

FIGURE 10-2 – CONTRACT BOOKLET

Chapter Ten: Integrating Interventions 109

Contract

Name _____

Goal	Time	Mon	Tue	Wed	Thu	Fri	Total
	 🕐						
	 🕐						
	 🕐						
	 🕐						
	 🕐						
	 🕐						

Total

FIGURE 10-3 – DESKTOP CONTRACT FORM

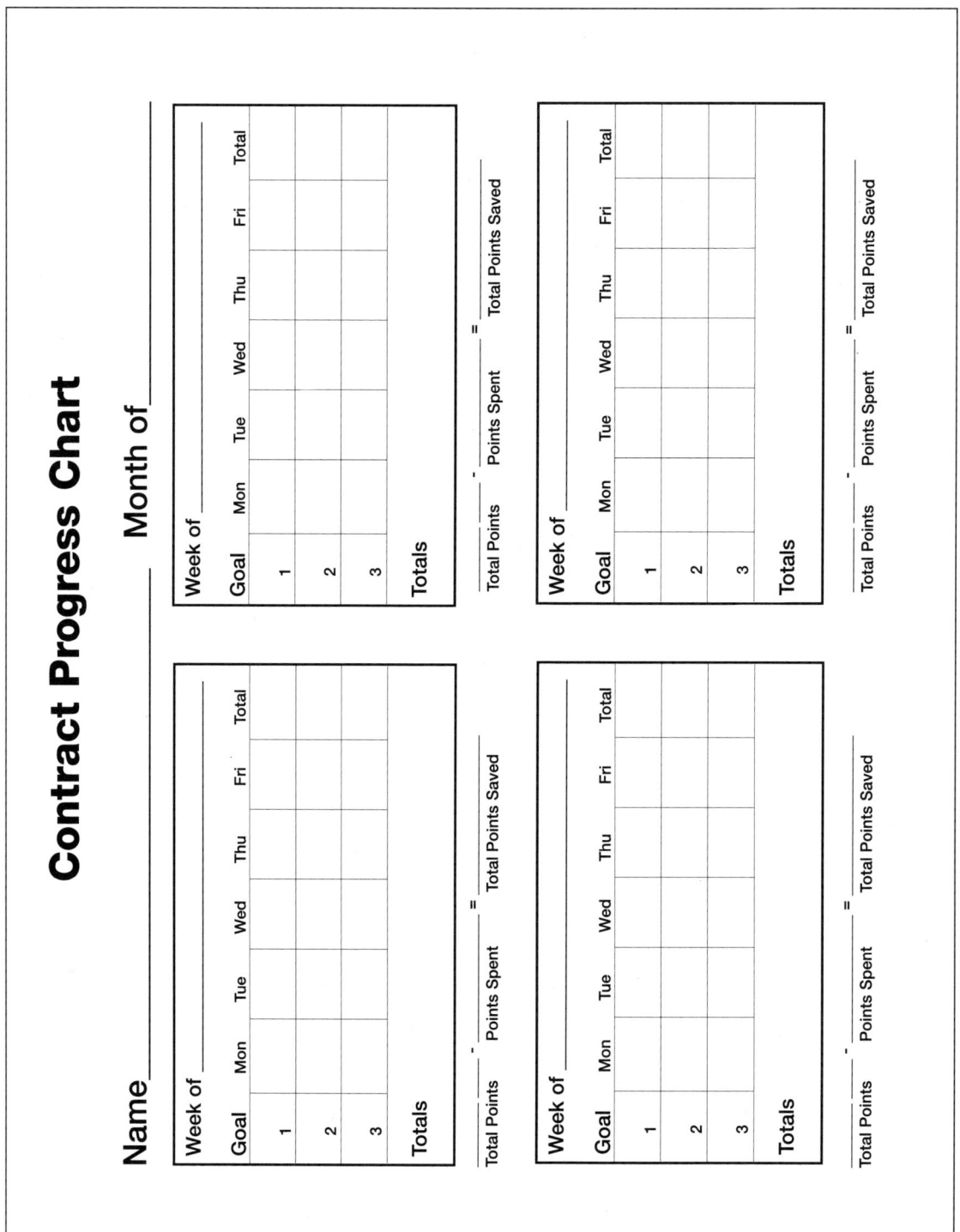

FIGURE 10-4 – CONTRACT SUMMARY CHART

Prize List

Name _____

Prize   **Points**

_____   _____

_____   _____

_____   _____

_____   _____

_____   _____

_____   _____

_____   _____

_____   _____

_____   _____

_____   _____

_____   _____

Figure 10-5 – Reinforcer Menu

When I use this approach in a mental health setting, my role is a little different, in that I spend more time teaching parents how to follow through on the reinforcement of desired behavior. I am still involved in the contract negotiation and establishment of the reinforcement menu. But the parent is responsible for awarding tokens and then exchanging the tokens for tangible rewards at the agreed upon intervals. I usually monitor both the parents' and child's progress in the program during the contract check segment of the session.

It should be obvious that, in this case, there is no real integration of play therapy with the behavior modification procedure. The two interventions are simply used concurrently to address different components of the same problem. The integration is more in the intended outcome: abatement of the behavioral symptom and resolution of the internal source of the symptom. A more integrated application of play therapy with behavioral approaches is provided next.

PLAY THERAPY AND AN INTEGRATED BEHAVIORAL INTERVENTION

Behavioral rehearsal is a common cognitive-behavioral approach rooted in social learning theory (Meichenbaum, 1977). In behavioral rehearsal, a child practices a desired behavior and receives reinforcement from the therapist, who is also acting as the child's behavioral "coach." Reinforcers can be tangible, such as food or tokens, or intangible, such as encouragement by the therapist. Usually a combination of both tangible and intangible reinforcers is used. One of the elements of behavioral rehearsal that is different in play therapy is the use of fantasy or pretends instead of real life situations. This means that the behavioral rehearsal will be constructed around puppets, dolls, or other toys, but the actual situation being rehearsed has a one-to-one correspondence with the real life situation in which the child needs to develop skills. This use of fantasy has the advantage of utilizing children's natural propensity to play, circumvents clients' defensiveness about targeted behaviors, and incorporates an element of creativity and fun into the rehearsal situation. The direct connection between the rehearsal and the real life situation is made by the therapist at the end of the rehearsal, with subsequent homework assignments related to practicing the skill.

The steps in implementing a behavioral rehearsal are: prepare the client, introduce the situation, take the client's role in the pretend to present the targeted behavior, move the client into the client role as you coach, reinforce accurate replication of the behavior, discuss the pretend, have the client rehearse the behavior directly with reinforcement, and encourage application of the skill outside of the playroom.

Preparing the Client

Initiating a behavioral rehearsal intervention is usually a shift from the less directive exploratory stage requiring some preparation of the client. If I know that this will be part of the game plan for a succeeding session, I prepare the client by saying, "Next time we are going to do something a little different. We are going to do a pretend for a few minutes before you start playing."

Introducing the Rehearsal

At the beginning of the next session, I introduce the behavioral rehearsal.

"Remember that I told you last week that we were going to do something different today? We are going to do a pretend for the first part of your time, then you will have your regular play time."

Then, I introduce the actual situation and construct the rehearsal with the child.

"Now we are going to do a pretend. For the past few sessions, you have been playing through situations about how other kids tease you. We're going to do a pretend today with some dolls about what to do when kids tease. You pick out the figures you want to use and tell me who they are supposed to be, and then we'll get started."

Note that I give the client the choice of what dolls to use and which characters the dolls will play. I begin the pretend by taking the role that represents the client; that is, the character who is being teased.

Counselor:	Who is going to be doing the teasing?
Client:	*This boy and this boy (indicates the dolls).*
Counselor:	So, this girl is going to be getting teased.
Client:	*Ya.*
Counselor:	Okay, I'll pretend for the girl, and you be the boys who are teasing her.
Client:	*I don't know.*
Counselor:	Think of what kids do to tease you and have them do it.
Client:	*(Holding boy dolls as he talks.) You're stupid. Geek, geek, geek, geek. You're a stupid geek.*
Counselor:	(Holding the girl doll.) You're right. I'm a stupid geek. You got me that time.
Client:	*But she agreed with them.*
Counselor:	That's right. Now what are they going to say?
Client:	*She can't agree with them.*
Counselor:	Why not?
Client:	*Because they're making fun of her.*
Counselor:	Try making fun of her some more and see what happens.
Client:	*(For dolls again.) You're a stupid fat geek.*
Counselor:	(As girl doll.) A stupid fat geek. Right again. (Speaking aloud to herself.) I think I will see if there's anything I can do for the teacher. (Doll walks over to adult doll that counselor is holding.) Teacher, can I help you with something?
Client:	*She should tell the teacher.*
Counselor:	She could, but if she did what would the boys do? Etc.

Move the Client into the Client Role

The next step is having the client take the role of the character that is modeling the desired behavior.

Counselor:	Let's do this again, but this time, you be the girl, and I'll be the teaser boys. I want you to do just what I did with the boys.
Client:	*I don't remember.*
Counselor:	That's not a problem – I'm going to help when you forget. Ready? (Holds boy dolls and teases client). Hey geeky girl. You're really stupid.
Client:	*(Holding girl doll.) Oh ya. You're stupid!*
Counselor:	Hold it. Is that what the girl said before?
Client:	*No.*
Counselor:	What did she say?
Client:	*You said...*
Counselor:	No, she said – make her say it to them (indicating the boy dolls).
Client:	*(As girl doll.) That's right, I'm a stupid geeky girl.*
Counselor:	Geek, geek, geeky girl.
Client:	*A geek, geek, geek, girl. You're absolutely right.*
Counselor:	Now what do you want to have her do?
Client:	*Oh. I'm going to go tell the teacher.*
Counselor:	Did she tell the teacher? Etc.

Reinforcing the Targeted Behavior

Finally, I reinforce the behavior, usually using a token type system. The simplest way to do this is to make checks on an index card for that day as the client replicates the behavior in the pretend. At the end of the practice, the client then chooses a reward from the counselor's standard reinforcer list.

Counselor:	We're going to do this one more time with you playing the girl. This time, I'm going to give you a check on this card every time you use the tricks I showed you. Ready?
Client:	*Who sees the card?*
Counselor:	This is just for me and you. When you are done, we'll see how many checks you have. Any other questions?
Client:	*No.*
Counselor:	(Holds boy dolls and teases client). Hey geeky girl. You're really stupid.
Client:	*(As girl doll.) That's right, I'm a stupid geeky girl.*
Counselor:	(Makes check on card in client's view.)
Counselor:	Geek, geek, geeky girl.
Client:	*A geek, geek, geek, girl. You're absolutely right.*
Counselor:	(Makes another check on card in client's view.) Etc.
Counselor:	(After completing practice.) Wow! You earned five checks. You did so well you earned a prize. Let's pick one from my prize list.

Discuss Application of the Skill

Once the pretend is completed, I process the behavioral rehearsal with the client. I use this time to understand the client's reaction to the rehearsal, to adapt the skill to the client's style, and to encourage the client to practice the skill in classroom situations.

Counselor:	So, what do you think about the way the girl took care of those guys?

Client:	*It's okay.*
Counselor:	Do you have any questions about it?
Client:	*Why didn't she tell the teacher?*
Counselor:	What do you think would happen if she told the teacher?
Client:	*The teacher would have yelled at them.*
Counselor:	What happens when you tell the teacher?
Client:	*She tells me not to tattle.*
Counselor:	And what do the kids who are bothering you do?
Client:	*They bother me more.*
Counselor:	So, telling the teacher wouldn't have helped the girl. That's why she did something different. She moved closer to the teacher to get away from the boys. And instead of tattling, she just tried to keep busy by helping the teacher. Etc.

DIRECT CLIENT PRACTICE

After the pretend has been discussed, I have the client rehearse the behavior directly, without the help of toys, using the same procedure that was used with the pretend. First, I play the client's role, with the client being the teaser. Then, I have the client practice the skill and I take the teaser's role. I again reinforce the client for accurate approximation of the behavior as we work through this rehearsal.

ENCOURAGE THE CLIENT TO USE THE SKILL

When the practice is complete, the child shifts to a regular play therapy session. However, the reinforcing isn't finished. If the child makes up a pretend in which the targeted behavior can be used, I will use directive intervention responses to encourage the child to utilize the skill, and then make a check on the index card. The child can again choose a reward at the end of the session based on the number of checks earned.

This procedure can and probably should also be combined with the behavior modification procedure described in the previous section. This can be done by contracting with the child to use the new skill in classroom situations, and having the teacher provide reinforcement using that procedure.

A METAPHORICAL STORYTELLING INTERVENTION

The use of metaphors in psychotherapy is usually connected with the Utilization approach of Milton Erickson (Haley, 1967). Metaphorical stories incorporate "themes that utilize the patient's experiences, resources, and mental maps" (Gunnison, 1999). When a metaphorical story is told to a client, the client is left to attach meaning to the metaphor, thus determining what aspect or experience is accessed and how it is used. Metaphors, in fact, give clients a great deal of control in the therapeutic process, which is especially important and useful with resistant clients. When a metaphor is used, the client ultimately has the choice to use it immediately in the session, think about it and use it after the session, or reject it completely (Whitaker & Bumberry, 1988). The power resides with the client.

Play therapy by its very nature is a metaphorical approach, and there is a relatively long history of using metaphorical stories in play therapy (Gardner, 1971). Thus, introducing such stories as more directive interventions is consistent with most play therapy approaches. How the story is introduced to the counseling situation depends on the therapeutic approach, the skills of the therapist, and the developmental level and abilities of the child. One thing that is certain is that the counselor needs to be comfortable enough with storytelling to incorporate some dramatic flair into the story, in order to maintain the client's interest; and must be creative enough to formulate a story that is child-appropriate and contains the message that the counselor desires to communicate in the metaphor. Not everyone can do this. If you find yourself struggling with creating the story, there are books, such as Mills's and Crowley's (1986) *Therapeutic Metaphors for Children and the Child Within* that provide metaphorical stories for common counseling situations with children. If you find that drama is not your cup of tea, there are audiotapes of metaphorical stories that can be played for children. If all else fails, you can always rely on traditional favorites which were actually created to serve as metaphors for children of previous generations. For instance, "The Three Pigs" is a common story I use with children and families where safety issues are tantamount. "Hansel and Gretel" is a great metaphor for what we now call "stranger danger."

There are a number of permutations to metaphorical storytelling, such as mutual storytelling (Gardner, 1971), the creative characters technique (Brooks, 1981), and Ericksonian metaphors. The important thing to keep in mind is that the use of metaphors involves the client in a three stage process of recognizing the metaphor as an event that deviates from the routine responses of the counselor, deciding that the metaphor is not meaningless, and consequently, attaching meaning to the metaphor (Sledge, 1977). Specificity of the symbols is necessary for the metaphor to be useful to the client (Sledge). Therefore, when constructing metaphors for children, it is particularly important to use symbols that are concrete and familiar to the client.

Two examples of metaphorical stories are provided here, one using concrete symbols of puppets, and the other, a straightforward story that is told by the therapist. In both types of metaphorical storytelling the counselor follows similar steps in developing the story.

> 1. The counselor defines what issue the metaphor will address.
> 2. The counselor outlines the story, including characters or toys that the client has used consistently in the play therapy. At this point the counselor also decides about how much of the story will involve direct client input, and how much will be therapist directed.
> 3. The counselor tells the story to the client.
> 4. The counselor asks the client what the story meant to him or her immediately after the session.
> 5. In the following session, the counselor asks the client if he or she thought about the story and had any additional thoughts or reactions to it since the last session.

As I indicated above, I like to involve clients in developing the stories. This occurs to different degrees depending on the age and developmental level of the child, and the purpose of the story. I typically develop most of the story when working with younger children and children who are cognitively limited. I might include a few decision points in the story at which the client needs to make a choice between two alternatives. With older children and children who can think more abstractly, I often develop the central theme of the story and ask the client for more substantial input into the development of the story. The second story below is an example of the former, while the first story illustrates the latter.

TRACY: THE TALE OF A FISH

One approach to making metaphors more concrete is by using props, such as dolls, puppets, and sand. In fact, there is an entire sub-field of play therapy that focuses on sandplay (Allen & Berry, 1987; Vinturella & James, 1987), while the use of puppets has been a common feature of many play therapy approaches (Carter, 1987; James & Myer, 1987). The story that is discussed in this section is an example of the use of puppets in an intervention.

Tracy was a nine-year-old female who was exhibiting significant anger management problems and defiance. Tracy didn't just become angry, she became enraged. And when she became enraged, there were no limits to what she might do. At various times she had intentionally pushed her mother down, run down her street blindly until she was lost, and kicked holes in walls in her house. Tracy was also resistant to counseling, refusing to do anything during some sessions, and refusing to speak directly to me during most sessions. When she had interacted with me, Tracy disclosed a love of dolphins. After a session of Tracy refusing to participate in therapy, I decided to construct a metaphorical story about anger management to be used during the next episode of resistance. Using my old DUSO Dolphin puppet (Dinkmeyer, 1973) and a killer whale puppet, I was prepared to tell my story.

Tracy started the next session refusing to enter the playroom when directed to do so by her mother. Tracy stood outside the door, waiting for me to engage her in a power struggle to enter my room. Instead, I sat at my desk busying myself and told Tracy she could choose to enter my room when she was ready or choose not to. After approximately 700 hours (which was actually five minutes), Tracy entered the playroom and lay down on the sofa covering her face with her arms. I again told her that she could choose to begin when she was ready. After an additional 900 hours (15 minutes), I decided to implement my metaphorical story intervention. So, I put the puppets on my hands and began.

Counselor: I would like to tell you a story, Tracy. Is that okay?
Tracy: (No response.)
Counselor: Since you aren't talking to me, I think that means yes. Once upon a time there was a little dolphin named...what should I name the dolphin? I'm not really sure what to call it. Hum.
Tracy: (Peeking from under her arms) Sally.
Counselor: Sally. Sally had a big problem. You see every time Sally got angry, she would get herself in trouble. And I don't mean just little trouble, I mean big, big trouble. And the problem was that Sally got angry lots and lots of times – not just once a month or once a week, or even once a day. She got angry many times a day. If Mama Dolphin asked Sally to do something, Sally got angry (act this out with the dolphin puppet). If Sally didn't get her way, she stomped her fin on the ocean floor and screamed a dolphin scream. And when this happened, Mama Dolphin would send Sally to her cave, first for an hour, then for two hours, then for the whole rest of the day. (Act this out with puppets.) How do you think Sally felt when this happened.
Tracy: (Still peeking) Mad.
Counselor: How else do you think she felt?
Tracy: Sad.
Counselor: That's right, she felt very sad – so sad, she just didn't know what to do. What do you think she should do?
Tracy: I don't know.
Counselor: Well neither did she. One day Sally wanted a shrimp cream cone. That's just like an ice cream for dolphins. Sally really, really wanted a shrimp cream cone, but Mama Dolphin said no. Sally

	whined and begged, but Mama Dolphin said no. What do you think happened?
Tracy:	*(Arms off of face and watching, now.) Sally got mad.*
Counselor:	That's right. She got really, really mad. She got so mad that she swelled up and felt like she was going to burst. She got so mad that she didn't know what to do with herself. So, she started swimming away from the cave as fast as she could. She swam and swam and swam until she couldn't swim anymore (Acted out dolphin puppet swimming around the room, under tables, over shelves, etc.). Finally, she was so tired of swimming, she had to stop. And you know what?
Tracy:	*What?*
Counselor:	Sally realized that she was completely lost. She had been so mad that she paid no attention where she was going. She had no idea where she was. So, she began to cry. She had been crying for quite a while when she thought she heard a voice.

"Who's there?" she asked.
"It's just me," the voice replied.
"Who are you?" Sally asked again.
"I'm down here – the big shell. I'm Grandpa Clam."
Sally looked down and saw a huge shell on the ocean floor, with two eyes peering out.
"Please don't hurt me," she said meekly.
"I wouldn't hurt you – I'm just an old clam. You look very sad. Is something wrong?"
Sally told the story of her tantrum and how she ended up lost in a part of the ocean she never saw before. Grandpa Clam listened quietly and thought. You see it takes clams many, many years to get as large as he was. So, he was very old and had learned a lot of things in his lifetime. When Sally was done, Grandpa Clam spoke. "It sounds like you have a big, big problem when you get upset. And it's not only when you get mad. It's when you feel almost anything. When you feel sad, you act mad. When you feel scared, you act mad. I'll bet you even act mad when you feel happy. And now look at the pickle you're in! I've seen this thing before with some of the younger clams, and I think I can help, but you have to ask for help, if you want it."
As soon as Sally heard this, she felt mad again. She wasn't going to ask that big old shell for help. And so she just said nothing.
"Going to clam up, are you?" said Grandpa Clam, "Well, it's time for my nap then." And he closed his shell and began to snore.
Sally began to panic. "What am I going to do?" she thought. "I can't get back home, and I'm here all alone – except for this clam. I'm desperate." And so she knocked on Grandpa Clam's shell and said, "Grandpa Clam, wake up. I need help. I don't know what to do."
"Who's there? What's this?" Grandpa Clam said with a start.
"It's me, Sally, and I do want help, I really do."
"You do...you're sure, now? What I tell you won't work unless you are absolutely sure," said the clam.

"I'm sure, I'm really sure."
"Okay, then," said Grandpa Clam. "It's obvious to me that magic bubbles will help. You need magic bubbles."
"Where do I get them?" Sarah asked.
"You have them, you just don't know it. You spend so much of your time getting mad, that you don't even know you have these magic bubbles," said Grandpa Clam. "This is what you do to find them. Whenever you feel yourself getting mad, you get the magic bubbles. How do you know when you are getting mad?"
(Counselor aside to Tracy.) What do you think Sally feels when she gets mad – do her muscles get tight, or her head feels swollen? What do you think?

Tracy: Her head feels like it's gonna explode.

Counselor: (Back to story.) So, Sally replied, "My head feels like it's going to explode."
"Good, good," Grandpa Clam replied, "So when your head feels like it's going to explode, you get your magic bubbles."
"How?" Sally asked.
Grandpa Clam explained, "As soon as you notice your head feeling that way, you swim as fast as you can to the surface and take a deep breath. Then hold it for a minute and let yourself float slowly down beneath the surface. As you sink more and more, slowly blow air out so it makes bubbles. Those are the magic bubbles. The more you blow out, the calmer you will feel. By the time you float down to your home, you will be calm and able to listen to the other dolphins, even if you don't like what you hear. Try it now."
So, Sally practiced making magic bubbles the way Grandpa Clam had told her. (Counselor acts out with puppet.)
(Aside to Tracy.) Would you like to try making magic bubbles in the air? You can practice with Sally.
(Has puppet practice with Tracy.)
(Continues with story.) After Sally had practiced a long time and felt very calm, Grandpa Clam asked, "Are you ready to go home?"
"Oh, yes!" Sally replied.
Grandpa Clam gave Sally directions back to her house, then said, "If you forget about the magic bubbles, just remember my name."
"What do you mean?" asked Sally.
"Well if you just switch the two middle letters in my name, it spells c-a-l-m. And that's what the magic bubbles do for you – they make you calm. And remember, it won't always be easy, but if you practice, the magic bubbles will help you control your temper."
And so, Sally was off, and when she arrived back home, her parents were very relieved, but also very angry with her. When they talked about her punishment, she started to feel mad, but she remembered the magic bubbles and was able to control her temper. And as time went on things got better and better. It wasn't always easy, but the magic bubbles helped.
What do you think about that story?

Tracy:	*It was good.*
Counselor:	Do you think the magic bubbles could help you?
Tracy:	*Maybe.*
Counselor:	Well, just think about it, and maybe you could CHOOSE to try using the magic bubbles when your head feels like it's going to explode, or you could CHOOSE not to. You see, it's up to you.

THE LITTLE LEAF: A TRANSITION STRATEGY

In Chapter Eight, I talked about the transference issue involving the client's difficulty disengaging from the counseling activity, either from being overstimulated or by continuing a play behavior after returning to the classroom or home. In these types of situations, transition activities at the end of the play session are used to help the child disengage. Metaphorical stories are one type of transition strategy that is useful. I learned the story that is provided in this section from my friend, Gunner, whom I discussed in earlier chapters. Gunner developed an approach called Hypnocounseling (Gunnison, 1990) which utilizes metaphors and induction techniques differently than traditional hypnosis or hypnotherapy. Gunner incorporates Erickson's induction techniques (Haley, 1976) into Hypnocounseling, which gives clients complete control when induction techniques are used. These techniques do not involve hypnosis or hypnotic trances. They are simply ways of "seeding the unconscious" (Whitaker & Bumberry, 1988) in order to help clients utilize their own internal resources.

The Little Leaf is a relaxation story that is useful for helping children decrease feelings of anxiety or stress. It provides a concrete symbol, the leaf, on which the child can focus as the therapist tells the story. Clients can also learn to tell themselves the story as a strategy for calming themselves in real life situations. Basically, it is very similar to bedtime stories that are used to relax children and lull them to sleep. For all these reasons, I have found this story to be useful with children who tend to become overstimulated in play therapy sessions.

The steps for utilizing this intervention are the same as those for using any other story with one exception. The delivery of the story is less dramatic, but does require that the counselor use voice modulation as a technique for inducing relaxation. This requires that the counselor use a singsong type of intonation, alternating the tone from high to medium to low, and the volume from moderate to whispers. Emphasis is also placed on certain key words, which in the example will be capitalized. The rate of speech (pacing) is slow and deliberate, and needs to match the client's responses. For instance, if the client begins to breathe slowly, the counselor might state, "You might even find yourself breathing very SLOWLY and DEEPLY." For a more thorough description of this technique see Gunnison (1990). The story below is told in the counselor's voice.

We're going to do something a little different today. Remember, we talked about how you tend to be too excited after your session, and then get in trouble in your room. Well today we are going to take some time out now, so you will be CALM and RELAXED when you get back to your room. Ready?

I want you to get COMFORTABLE in your chair. You might CHOOSE to place your hands in your lap, or put your head down on the table, or NOT. (Pause)

I am going to tell you a story, and as you sit and LISTEN, you may CHOOSE to close your eyes, or not. (Pause)

Once upon a time there was a little leaf. He was a very happy little leaf who loved to hang out with his brother and sister leaves on a big maple tree in the woods. (Pause)

He especially enjoyed the FEELING of BLOWING GENTLY in the wind. (Pause) SWAYING back-and-forth and back-and-forth, until he was almost ASLEEP. (Pause)

He played like this through the spring and into summer, all the time just SWAYING in the BREEZE, until fall came. Well you know what happens to leaves in fall, and as the weather became COOLER and COOLER, the little leaf's brothers and sisters let go of their perches on the tree, and FLOATED GENTLY to the ground. SWIRLING in the breeze they floated DOWN, DOWN, DOWN. (Pause)

The little leaf felt very lonely, and wanted to join his brothers and sisters. So, one WINDY day, he closed his eyes very tightly, loosened his grip, and JUMPED from the tree. and before he knew it, the wind had PICKED HIM UP and carried him UP, UP, UP, into the COOL AIR. (Pause)

Then the little leaf began floating DOWN, DOWN, DOWN, floating in the breeze DOWN, DOWN, DOWN. (Pause)

And you may notice that your eyes are looking UP as if you can SEE the leaf floating. Or your eyes may be looking DOWN watching the leaf floating DOWN, DOWN, DOWN. (Pause)

And so the wind carried the leaf UP and then DOWN, GENTLY, GENTLY, GENTLY. (Pause) DOWN, DOWN, DOWN. And you may see the leaf FLOATING down. Or you may see nothing. (Pause)

Or you may FEEL as if you are FLOATING like the leaf. Or you may just feel COMFORTABLE and RELAXED. I don't know. It's your CHOICE. (Pause)

And the leaf floated DOWN and watched as he came closer and closer to the ground. SLOWLY and GENTLY floating in the AIR. (Pause)

DOWN (Pause), DOWN (Pause), DOWN (Pause) he went, SLOWLY approaching the ground. (Pause)

And then the leaf landed in a pile of leaves, like landing on a giant, SOFT, STUFFED, pillow. (Pause) So soft that he sank into the pillow for a few moments. (Pause)

And then he felt RELAXED (pause), and CONTENT (pause), and SAFE (pause), and almost SLEEPY. (Pause) Glad to be with his brothers and sisters again.

And you might even feel a little SLEEPY, now, or not. (Pause for a minute or so.)

And now, remaining RELAXED and CONTENT, you will begin to feel more alert as I count to three. One, your feet and legs are feeling more alert. (Pause) Two, your body is feeling more alert. (Pause) Three, your arms, neck and head are feeling more alert. And as you sit there you will open your eyes and feel ALERT, RELAXED, and CONTENT.

Now when you return to class, you will continue to feel relaxed and alert, go to your desk, sit down and join the class.

The thing to keep in mind is that using stories requires planning and practice – it's not something that most folks can do off the tops of their heads. You need to have a clear idea of the purpose of the story, the message you are going to communicate, the story outline, and the way you want to dramatize the story. If you use puppets or sand, you also have to feel comfortable with this media and know how to use it in a way that is believable to children. With practice, your skills should improve, and you should begin to feel more relaxed and confident about using storytelling.

Summary

This chapter provided just a few examples of interventions that can be incorporated into the play therapy process. There are many types of interventions that can be utilized with play therapy. Doing so simply requires some thought regarding how to interface with the particular play therapy approach being used, and when in the process the intervention can be appropriately implemented.

Homework

Since storytelling is a particularly useful intervention, your homework for this chapter is to develop a metaphorical story for a client with whom you are presently working. Once you develop the story, practice it. It is also useful to practice with a professional colleague or friend, as they will be able to provide feedback on how you might improve the story. Use the outline below for planning purposes. Then respond to the follow-up questions to evaluate this experience.

Story Planning Form

Problem or Issue: _____

Metaphor being used: _____

Remember: Choose symbols that are attractive or interesting to the client.

Props to be used, if any (puppets, etc.) _____

Outline of the Story: _____

_____
_____
_____
_____
_____
_____
_____
_____
_____
_____
_____
_____
_____

Follow-up Procedures (behavior modification, etc.) _____

_____
_____
_____

STORYTELLING INTERVENTION SELF-EVALUATION

1. How did the client react to the story?

2. Did the client seem to connect with or understand the metaphor:

    Immediately? How?

    Later? How?

    Not at all?

3. What do you think you did well in implementing the intervention?

4. What do you think you need to improve?

5. Rate your comfort level with storytelling.

    1   2   3   4   5
    Very Uncomfortable   Very Comfortable

Chapter 11

Termination

Termination, as the final stage of the play therapy process, stimulates some unique issues, to the extent that I feel a need to pay particular attention to this stage. While the idea of ending therapy because the work is done should be seen as a triumph for the child, it can just as readily be perceived as a rejection of the child by the counselor, if the message is not communicated appropriately. That is, the counselor's communication of, "You don't need to see me anymore," can be perceived by the child as, "I don't want to see you anymore." Thus, it is very important to approach termination as a sub-process that requires specific procedures to be implemented by the counselor. This brief chapter will outline issues, determining factors, and procedures in the termination process.

Determining if a Client is Ready to Terminate

Determining whether or not a client is ready to end play therapy is a function of whether or not specific problems and needs that were presented at the outset of counseling have been dealt with, and general goals of play therapy met. Specific determinants include symptom remission (Henderson, 1987; Landreth, 1991; O'Connor, 1991), developmental needs and use of defenses (Landreth), and shifts in the family system (Cerio, 1994). General determinants include level of self esteem, stress tolerance, and personal responsibility (Landreth).

Symptom Remission. The big question to ask with any client, adult or child, is, have the presenting symptoms abated (without being replaced by other symptoms)? If the child presents an externalizing type problem -that is, acts out – then observable behavioral improvement is the benchmark for termination. With children who are internalizers, exhibiting disturbances in mood, improvement in mood is the determining factor for termination.

How you determine this is an issue unto itself. Unfortunately, due to time constraints, many counselors simply make this judgment on their own without much feedback from individuals with whom the child has contact. If counselors do seek feedback, they tend to use anecdotal or subjective evaluations from teachers and parents. Although this might be valid with children who exhibit obvious problems and where the play therapy is the only change in the child's environment, such as in the case of the compulsive hair puller described by Barlow, Strother, and Landreth (1985), it presents validity and reliability problems with children who exhibit more common behavioral difficulties. Such subjective feedback is influenced by the Hawthorne effect (Gay, 1976): the tendency by others to perceive positive change because they know an intervention is being used. A much more valid and reliable method for assessing symptom remission is use of an empirically validated behavior rating scale as pre- and post therapy measures of behavior (Cerio, 1999). Newer rating scales, such as the Behavior Assessment System for Children (Reynolds & Kamphaus, 1992), are designed to assess multiple internalizing and externalizing behaviors, incorporate validity scales as checks for extremes in ratings, and have been standardized on large, representative populations of children, parents, and teachers.

Thus, the information obtained through these scales is much more objective and less likely to be subject to the Hawthorne effect. If a child is rated as exhibiting decreases in problem behaviors or moods based on a pre-determined criterion, then a counselor can conclude that the child has improved.

While use of objective information is a good practice, it is not always possible due to the type of presenting problem. For instance, with children who have been sexually abused, the symptoms might be so specific, such as anxiety responses when reminded of the abuse, that others might not even be aware that the child is experiencing distress. In these situations, the counselor's assessment of the child's therapeutic behavior is critical in determining the appropriateness of termination. The counselor needs to be aware of issues the child discusses and metaphors that are repeated during the course of therapy. For instance, I have observed that children who have been sexually abused tend to move from metaphors of danger and helplessness (snakes or alligators attacking dolls) to metaphors of strength and safety (the dolls defeating the attackers). This is usually accompanied by similar shifts in their verbalizations. So, I consider this shift in therapeutic behavior as part of my assessment of progress.

Developmental Needs. Clients also enter therapy with specific developmental needs, such as needs for nurturing, independence, or initiative-taking. If these needs are significantly discrepant with a client's chronological age and level of cognitive functioning, then the effectiveness of meeting these needs through therapy is another consideration for termination. The counselor must first determine whether or not it is even possible to meet such needs through therapy. For instance, if the home and school environments are relatively stable, then it is possible that a child will be able to work through these needs in therapy. However, if, for instance, the child's family is unable to meet such needs at home, it is less likely that therapy can be successful in this endeavor.

Changes in the Family System. This area is closely linked to the two areas discussed above. The child functions in a reciprocal relationship with caregivers (Minuchin & Fishman, 1981), in that, changes in the child inevitably will cause changes in other members of the family and vice versa. If the child's symptom or behavior functions as a stabilizing mechanism in the family, then it is less likely that the child's behavior will improve as a result of individual counseling. That is, symptom remission actually threatens the stability of the family, thus, family members will either consciously or unconsciously undermine the client's improvement. This same type of relationship exists between the child and teachers, principals, and other adults in the child's world. It is important, then, for the counselor to have at least a vague idea that the system in which the child functions has responded to the change in the child in a way that supports any progress the child has made.

What do you look for in this respect? Some things I look for include:

- Statements from parents and teachers that are encouraging to the child.
- Changes in adult behavior that complement the child's changes.
- A decrease in negative statements from adults about the child.
- A positive change in adults' perceptions of the child.

Use of Defenses. Children who are upset or frequently in trouble usually learn to use certain strategies as ways to protect their rather fragile self esteem. These can be the more classic type of defenses, such as repression or denial, as might be observed with traumatized children who exhibit symptoms but cannot recall the traumatizing event. Or they can be more obvious responses, such as automatically blaming others for difficulties in anticipation of being blamed; giving up without trying in anticipation of failing; and physically or verbally attacking others in anticipation of being attacked, to name a few. For the purpose of determining the appropriateness of termination, I look for a decrease or absence of the client's use of these types of defenses, without substitution of other defenses.

Self Esteem. There is a body of literature that suggests that children who are involved in play therapy show improvement in levels of self esteem, no matter what the specific presenting symptoms are (Axline, 1947; Bleck & Bleck, 1982; Carmichael, 1991; Crow, 1994; Gilmore, 1971; Glass, 1987; Griffiths, 1971; Swartz & Swartz, 1985). Thus, it seems reasonable to expect and assess such improvement when determining progress in therapy. As is true with symptom remission, this assessment may be conducted through subjective observations of clients' self-statements, risk taking, and perseverance; or more empirically through standardized self esteem measures, both self-reports and informant reports.

Stress Tolerance. As a child's mood and behavior improves, it can be expected that her coping skills will also improve. That is, if a child is showing improvement in symptoms and is less defensive, the child should exhibit more resilience when things aren't going her way. Thus, one area I also weigh when considering termination, is both the child's and significant adults' reports of the child's responses to stresses in the child's life. In general, another benchmark of improvement is clients being more effective in coping with some of the stressors in their lives.

Personal Responsibility. Child-centered play therapists, such as Landreth, emphasize the child's development of personal responsibility as a goal of play therapy. What this means is that the child shows a willingness to take initiative, make choices, and accept the consequences of these choices. At the point of termination, this is something that you would want to observe happening within the play therapy situation *and* receive reports from others that this is happening outside of the therapeutic setting.

Issues

There are a few common issues of which counselors must be aware when decisions to terminate have been made. These include client feelings of rejection and abandonment; recapitulation of issues; and client and counselor feelings of dependency and loss.

Rejection and Abandonment. As alluded to above, telling clients that they no longer need to see you can be perceived as a rejection, even when the therapeutic relationship is a solid one. This may be a particularly important issue with clients who have been abandoned by caregivers, such as foster children and adopted children; clients who have attachment issues with caregivers, such as children whose parents are rejecting; clients who have separation and control issues, such as children in divorce situations; and clients who have general trust issues with adults, such as abused children. There is no way to avoid these issues when terminating. So, the issues must be incorporated into the termination process, and the termination should be used as a "teaching moment." The lesson that the therapist wants the client to learn is that finishing the counseling process DOES NOT mean that the relationship ends. It means that the relationship changes, and this change means that it will be maintained in a different way. The procedures outlined below are designed to communicate this message.

Recapitulation of Issues. Yalom (1985) pointed out that when termination is imminent, clients will sometimes "backslide" and begin exhibiting symptoms or behaviors that had long ago abated. It is almost like the client has to make one last effort to keep the relationship going. This is not an unusual phenomenon to observe in play therapy. Children will sometimes return to aggressive or limit testing behaviors that were characteristic of an earlier part of the process. Or they will manufacture complaints or problems that don't really exist. Some backsliding is normal and should be expected once the client is told of the decision to terminate. The counselor's task is to remain committed to the decision and focused on the client's progress.

Client and Therapist Dependence and Loss. During the course of therapy, it is inevitable that BOTH the client and therapist develop a mutual dependence on each other. I am not talking here about the type of countertransference in which the therapist relies on the client as the crutch to maintain the therapist's feelings of well being. The type of dependence to which I refer is a normal component of therapeutic relationships, a mutual attraction or likableness. Even though the relationship will continue in a different form, this type of dependence must end with the counseling process, and this, in turn, fuels feelings of loss on both the counselor's and client's parts. Whitaker (Whitaker & Bumberry, 1988) called this "the empty nest" that the therapist must acknowledge and work through. Counselor awareness of this issue is important, as these feelings may cause some reluctance of the therapist to terminate counseling.

THE TERMINATION PROCESS

Most play therapy experts recommend that children require multiple sessions for termination (Jernberg, 1979; O'Connor, 1991). In general, I recommend that a minimum of three sessions be planned for termination in order to provide the client and counselor with adequate time to work through the types of issues discussed above. Children with less severe problems and few or no issues regarding relationships, may require only two sessions. Children with more severe problems, particularly the types of relationship issues outlined above, usually require more than three sessions. The process needs to be adapted to the client's needs. There are several components to termination, which are outlined below.

Preparation. Once the decision to terminate has been made, the first step is announcing it to the client. I typically do this at the beginning of what becomes the first termination session. At this time, I set a tentative date for the final session and have the child make something to use as a reminder of termination in succeeding sessions. What the child decides to make is his or her choice. Reminders usually take the form of a calendar, but I have also seen client's make such things as charts, bouquets of paper flowers, bunches of balloons, and (most guilt producing for me) a series of broken hearts. Some client's completely avoid making reminders, which is an acceptable choice. The counselor becomes the reminder in these cases.

Keep Focused on Termination. At the beginning of each session after the announcement, the counselor reminds the client that termination is near. Either at the beginning or the end of the session, the child crosses that session off the calendar or removes one of the reminders and counts how many more sessions are left. During the session, it is important that the counselor maintain the focus on termination and not play into denial. In some sense, this is a low level bereavement process for both the client and the counselor. Thus, it is not unusual to see some behaviors that parallel a true bereavement situation.

Expect Some Regression. As stated above, some recapitulation of issues is expected. You may see the reappearance of old problem behaviors or a rehashing of issues through symbolic play. It is also fairly normal to see the child express some anger and resentment toward the therapist through increased aggressive play, increased limit testing, or exclusion of the therapist from what previously had been relationship play. The therapist's task is to acknowledge and affirm the child's feelings as normal reactions to termination.

Emphasize Change. The counselor needs to focus on the client's growth and change during counseling. Seize opportunities to point out positive changes in behavior, mood, self esteem, and coping skills. I even like to incorporate Jernberg's (1979) techniques of illuminating the child's physical growth during the time period in which counseling has occurred. Since most children grow relatively fast, this is a readily available illustration of change.

Counselor Awareness of Feelings. Counselors need to be aware of their own feelings related to termination. It's normal to feel a little twinge of sadness when saying good-bye to a client. Share this with the child when appropriate. This not only helps the counselor disengage, it also models to the client self-disclosure of such feelings.

The Final Session. During the session before the final session, I have the client plan the final session. The plan includes choosing a snack and deciding on favorite activities that the client wants to play one last time. When the final session arrives, the client and I have a "party" to celebrate the client's success. Again, I focus on the client's progress in counseling and how the client will use his or her skills in the future. At the end of the session, I give the client a small present as a transitional object. This can be something as simple as a photo of the client and me, a stuffed animal, miniature lego kit, or diary. I choose a gift based on the age of the client and the type of activities that the client enjoys most in the therapy. In situations in which it is unlikely that the client will see me again, I also give the client a mailing address, should they want to write. This is part of the message that, although counseling is ending, the relationship will still continue in a different way.

In school settings, I often found myself suffering from "false termination." That is, I had to stop seeing clients at the end of the school year, even though counseling was not completed. I treated this situation as a normal termination process with one difference. In the last session, I left open the possibility that the client would continue with me the next year unless something changed during the summer that made it unnecessary or impossible for the client to continue. For instance, the client's family might move out of the district, or something might change in the client's situation that would result in resolution of the problem. I told clients that I would see them early in the next school year to determine if they were going to continue or not.

The things to keep in mind when you reach the point of terminating are:

1. Give the client and yourself enough time to transition out of counseling.
2. Be aware of issues and feelings that may arise that are unique to the client's situation.
3. Confront issues and feelings openly.
4. Encourage the client's independence – it's part of being a Good Mother.

Homework

At this point of the do-it-yourself course, you probably are working with one or two real clients. While you are likely not at the point of terminating, you can still plan ahead. Complete at least one of the following worksheets to help you think about the termination process with a client.

TERMINATION WORKSHEET

Client's First Name:_____

1. What is the client's presenting problem?

2. How will you determine the client's progress in counseling?

3. What specific client issues do you think will arise related to termination?

4. What counselor issues might arise related to termination?

5. How many sessions do you think you will need to terminate with this client?

6. What type of transitional object will be appropriate for this client?

TERMINATION WORKSHEET

Client's First Name:_____

1. What is the client's presenting problem?

2. How will you determine the client's progress in counseling?

3. What specific client issues do you think will arise related to termination?

4. What counselor issues might arise related to termination?

5. How many sessions do you think you will need to terminate with this client?

6. What type of transitional object will be appropriate for this client?

Chapter 12

Orienting the Consumer

"What is this play stuff?" "Why are you using it with kids here?" "Why does Johnny tell me that all he does is 'play' when he comes for counseling?" "Aren't you supposed to be talking to these kids when you counsel them?" "School counselors aren't supposed to be doing 'therapy.'" These are common questions and statements that play therapists hear. And they are important questions because they inform counselors about misconceptions about counseling.

Where do people learn about counseling and psychotherapy? When you think about it, the main source of information about counseling is the entertainment industry, particularly motion pictures and television. These outlets provide stereotypes, both negative and positive, of counseling professionals and the counseling process. The negative stereotypes typically portray counselors as "shrinks" who are waiting to analyze every word and action of an individual, or far-out gurus who are open to calling anything "therapy." Then there are the television and radio "psychologists," most of whom lack any formal training, and are only too willing to offer glib advice to viewers and listeners. The most evident positive stereotype is the portrayal of counselors as individuals who are brimming with wisdom, and of the counseling process as a series of dramatic breakthroughs. Even classic publications on play therapy, such as Axline's (1964) *Dibs in Search of Self,* contribute to these stereotypes. These are powerful misconceptions that adults carry with them when they seek counseling for themselves or refer children for therapy. And this presents big problems for real mental health workers who are "in the trenches." To paraphrase a statement of Carl Whitaker (1986), sometimes people come to therapy just to see what a real shrink looks like.

Play therapy, and any type of child counseling for that matter, cannot be conducted in a vacuum. Adults who are involved with the child impact the therapeutic process both positively and negatively. These same adults serve as referral sources, and if they have reservations about the counseling being provided, they will be reluctant to refer children to you. Thus, it is critical to educate adults about play therapy and its applications in the particular setting in which it is being used. The purpose of this chapter is to provide counselors with ideas for presenting orientations on play therapy to groups of adults who impact children: teachers, administrators, parents, caseworkers, and other counselors. My intention is to provide you with a variety of activities and materials for presentations, as well as tips for adapting these to the specific needs of various groups. The materials in this chapter are designed for immediate use and to be easily copied as handouts or transparencies. So, feel free to do so!

Counselor Goals

Before presenting any type of workshop, it is important for me to identify my personal goals for the participants. These goals differ from instructional objectives in that the former involves what I want to accomplish, while the latter involves what participants should learn. Thus, you might look at the counselor goals as the underlying, general purpose of the presentation.

Demystification. Like the magician who reveals how he does his tricks, one of my goals of any presentation is to take the mystery out of play therapy. I want people to understand that play therapy, like counseling with adults, is a gradual process that requires hard work and patience on the part of the counselor, client, and adults who impact the client. There are no smoke and mirrors, and, usually, no intense catharsis. I have found that if adults can understand play therapy for what it is – a communication modality for children that parallels talking therapy with adults – they are more accepting and less skeptical of the approach. I have very strong feelings about professionals who consciously attempt to maintain the aura of magic around play therapy. I see this as a self serving way to distance parents or teachers, and to maintain some sort of hierarchical position above other adults who are involved with the child.

Modifying Expectations. A second goal of orientation is to modify the expectations of the adults around the child; that is, to establish realistic expectations that are congruent with what actually happens in play therapy. This requires providing specific information about play therapy process, which can range from general information for consumers (parents, administrators) to specific skill training for other helping professionals (counselors, teachers). There is a whole body of research that demonstrates that accurate adult expectations of counseling have a positive impact on counseling process and outcomes with children (Day & Reznikoff, 1980; Holmes & Urie, 1975; Hoyt, 1979).

Recruiting Allies. A third underlying goal of mine is to begin developing relationships with adults who are more open to or interested in the play therapy approach. These are people who can serve as "allies" in the future in terms of utilizing my services, recommending me to others, and providing testimonials regarding children who have been helped through play therapy. While this might sound Machiavellian, it is a necessity within the political matrices of schools and agencies. The fact is that more support and referrals will come from these allies than any other source.

Your Goals. Take a few minutes now and list any underlying goals you may have for play therapy orientations in your work setting.

Goal 1: _____

_____

Goal 2: _____

_____

Goal 3: _____

_____

INSTRUCTIONAL OBJECTIVES AND TARGET GROUPS

Instructional objectives for presentations focus on what participants should learn and are more specific than goals. For the presentations that are being discussed here, the instructional objectives will be at least partially determined by the target group of the presentations. Hence, it makes sense to talk about these two areas together. Having done scores of presentations for groups ranging from boards of education to parents to teachers, I have some sense of the types of objectives that are appropriate for various groups of consumers. I have divided up objectives by target groups from most to least technical presentations.

Counselors, Psychologists, Social Workers, and Other Mental Health Professionals. Presentations for school and community mental health professionals might include any of the following objectives.

Participants will:
1. Understand the functions of play.
2. Understand the goals and functions of play therapy.
3. Develop skills for facilitative responding in play therapy.
4. Develop limitsetting skills.
5. Apply play therapy skills in (simulations, work setting, etc.).
6. Develop a working knowledge of play therapy process.
7. Compare and contrast conceptual frameworks for play therapy.
8. Conceptualize play therapy cases.

Teachers, Administrators, and Other Allied School and Health Professionals. Instructional objectives for these groups are usually less technical and less skill oriented. Participants will:

1. Understand the functions of play.
2. Understand the goals and functions of play therapy.
3. Understand the function of toys and activities used in play therapy.
4. Develop general awareness of play therapy process.
5. Understand their roles in the therapeutic process.
6. Understand the importance and limits of confidentiality in therapy.

Parents, Boards of Education, Community Groups, and Other Lay Persons. With lay individuals and groups, the objectives are similar to those for allied professionals except that they are not at all technical. These non-measurable educational objectives focus on simply increasing awareness.

Participants will:

1. Develop awareness of the goals and functions of play therapy.
2. Develop awareness of toys and activities used in play therapy.
3. Develop general awareness of play therapy process.
4. Understand their roles in the therapeutic process.
5. Understand the importance and limits of confidentiality in therapy.

Your Objectives. List the target group and objectives for the first play therapy presentation you would like to do after completing this book.

Target Group: _____

Objectives:

1. _____
   _____

2. _____
   _____

3. _____
   _____

4. _____
   _____

5. _____
   _____

INSTRUCTIONAL ACTIVITIES

As a teacher, I have been a longtime follower of the philosophy of John Dewey (1938), who believed that experience drove learning, and that through experience, individuals developed the "internal connections" (p. 91) that we call knowledge. This is the idea behind the activities I have included in this book. I also follow this philosophy in workshops and presentations, incorporating hands-on, experiential activities, rather than just talking about play therapy. I recommend that anyone presenting a program on play therapy do the same for a number of reasons. First, experiential activities provide participants with a more real sense of play therapy. Second, hands-on activities serve as learning anchors for concepts and skills that are discussed in the presentation. Third, practicing skills in a safe workshop environment with other professionals tends to increase participants' comfort levels for using the skills with children. Fourth, hands-on activities serve as icebreakers, relaxing participants, which allows them to focus more readily on the presentation material. Finally, these activities are fun.

In addition to experiential activities, there are other methods and procedures that may be incorporated into presentations. Videotape segments of play therapy provide participants with reality-based examples of play therapy process and skills. Demonstrations of particular skills provide participants with models for responding to particular play therapy situations. Anecdotes from those "allies" I spoke about above, are helpful with certain non-counselor target groups in providing perspectives other than the presenter's regarding the usefulness of play therapy. With more clinically-oriented professional groups, reviewing areas of play therapy research is helpful in illuminating empirical support for this approach.

There are a few other general issues you should keep in mind when making presentations – the do's and don'ts.

Do:
- Outline your presentation beforehand, including time requirements.
- Present information clearly.
- Use visuals, such as transparencies or Power Point type software.
- Involve participants whenever possible.
- Provide handouts for participants to follow, so they can listen without taking notes.
- Answer questions when asked.
- Be open to different and opposing perspectives.

Don't:
- Present yourself as a guru or all-knowing expert. No one really is.
- Wing it.
- Be afraid to admit you don't know something.
- Try to convince a hardcore skeptic. It's a no win situation.
- Just lecture without allowing for exchanges with participants.

Two examples of presentation outlines directed at different types of target groups are provided below.

EXAMPLE 1: A One-hour Teacher Orientation

Opening Activity (10 min.)
Teachers will circulate in groups of four to different stations, each of which has toys from one of the four toy groups.

Opening Demo (5 min.)
Role play of intrusive adult counselor.

Discussion (10 min.)
Functions of play.
What is play therapy?
With whom is it useful?

Video (10 min.)
"Techniques of Play Therapy" (first segment)

Demonstration (10 min.)
Functions of different types of toys.

Discussion (10 min.)
Confidentiality
Referral Process

Questions (5 min.)

Note that this is a relatively brief session, so none of the topics will be covered in any particular depth. The goal is to simply provide participants with a flavor for play therapy. I found that it was useful to pair this type of presentation with more in-depth follow up sessions that would provide interested teachers with a more substantive understanding of play therapy.

EXAMPLE 2: A Three-hour Counselor Workshop

Opening Activity (15 min.)
Unstructured play at play therapy stations.

Discussion (20 min.)
Functions of play.
What is play therapy?
With whom is it useful?
Theoretical roots.

Video (20 min.)
"Techniques of Play Therapy" (first 2 segments)
Process after.
Functions of play therapy.

Discussion (20 min.)
Toy selection and function.
Setting up the playroom.

Demonstration (10 min.)
The first session.

Discussion (20 min.)
Facilitative responding.
Therapist's role.

Activity (20 min.)
Facilitative responding practice video.

Activity (30 min.)
Simulations in dyads.
Process.

Discussion (15 min.)
Research on play therapy.

Questions (10 min.)

In this example, more time is devoted to each area to enable the presenter to provide more depth. There are also more participant involvement and practice, since professionals in this group would desire to utilize these skills with children. However, this workshop would still only be an introduction to the approach for this audience.

YOUR WORKSHOP

It's time again for you to work on the workshop you are going to present. Based on your work in the previous sections, you should now outline the activities you will incorporate to meet your objectives.

Type of Activity	Time Required	Activity Content
_____	_____	_____
_____	_____	_____
_____	_____	_____
_____	_____	_____
_____	_____	_____
_____	_____	_____
_____	_____	_____
_____	_____	_____

Desired Outcomes

How do you know that your presentation had the effect you desired on your audience? These are the outcomes you would like to see as a result of your efforts. Outcomes should be linked to the goals and objectives of the presentation. Ideally, the outcomes should be measurable and meaningful. But realistically, this is not always the case, especially in counseling-related areas. However, it is a good practice to incorporate some measurable outcomes that can help you determine if your efforts had any meaningful effect. Let's look at some examples of outcomes linked to objectives.

Awareness or Understanding of Play Therapy. Objectives, such as, "Participants will understand the function of play therapy," can be measured through what amounts to a traditional test of knowledge. This can be as simple as asking participants at the end of the presentation to answer the question, "What is play therapy," on a scrap sheet of paper, and hand it in to the presenter. The presenter can then determine how many of the participants responded correctly, and this percentage is the measurable outcome. A second method of measuring this outcome is to have participants respond to a number of statements about play therapy using a true-false format. This approach can be used to assess outcomes in several ways. The outcome could be the average number of correct responses. Or, a minimum criterion of correct responses could be set which a specified percentage of participants are expected to attain. Or, a difference score could be used. That is, the instrument could be administered as a pretest before the workshop and as a post-test after the workshop. In order for the workshop to be deemed effective, a certain average percentage increase in scores would be required.

Changing Expectations. Goals and objectives that focus on changing expectations can be measured in a similar way. Attitudinal scales such as one used by Cerio, Taggart, and Costa (1999) are a convenient way to measure beliefs and attitudes. Again, if you are interested in change, then such scales could be used as pre- and post-tests for the presentation or workshop. However, when we talk about meaningful change, what types of responses to the presentation would reflect positive changes in attitudes? One measure that I have used in the past has been an informal behavior tally. I often found teachers and administrators making unreasonable requests of me in relation to the therapy – the "talk to Suzy about..." scenario was one such example I used in Chapter Eight. So, one of my goals for an orientation session was to decrease such inappropriate requests and inappropriate comments. I measured this by simply tallying the number of these requests I received before the presentation. After the presentation, I would again track these requests for a similar period of time, my hope being that the number would decrease substantially. I felt that if a presentation or workshop were to have a true impact, then my main referral sources (the teachers) would be more realistic in their expectations, and more supportive of the counseling process.

General Effectiveness. Finally, I think a very simple way to measure general effectiveness of any counseling orientation workshop is to track the number and type of referrals. If I have been clear and effective in educating my consumers about an approach, they will probably want to use my services more often, and their reasons for referring children will be appropriate. Thus, a quantitative increase in referrals, and a qualitative improvement in the reasons for referral should indicate that the orientation had a positive impact.

There are many possible outcomes that can be measured for the type of presentations I have discussed in this chapter. You have to decide what fits your presentation and setting best, and what will help you determine if you had a meaningful impact or not. The examples above should simply serve as guides for this task.

YOUR OUTCOMES

Your final task in this chapter is to determine the outcomes you would like to achieve in your workshop. Go back and look at the objectives you stated above. Then, list outcomes that would indicate you accomplished your objectives below. Keep in mind that you want your outcomes to be measurable if possible.

Outcome 1

Outcome 2

Outcome 3

What is play?

Internal Energy source

Spontaneous

3 F's
- Fun: Play is pleasurable.
- Fantasy: Play allows kids to fantasize in a safe environment.
- Free: Play is conflict free.

Why do kids play?

Deal with experience through model situations.

Master reality through behavioral rehearsal.

Explore capacities through imitation and fantasy.

Process emotional conflict:
- Communication
- Expression of feelings
- Problem solving

Unifying principles of play therapy

- Philosophy of human closeness.
- Belief in child's ability to heal self.
- Unique setting of playroom.
- Permissiveness.
- Repetition compulsion.
- Transference/Countertransference.
- Regression.

What is play therapy?

Moustakas:
- A relationship between child and therapist
- Free expression
- Release of feelings

Axline:
- Playing out feelings and problems

Why use play therapy?

Erikson:
- Fundamental model of social development.

Axline:
- The natural medium of expression for the child.

Tasks/functions of play therapy

	INTERNAL		EXTERNAL	
	Task	**Function**	**Task**	**Function**
SPECIFIC	Positive Interaction with Client – PEGS. Identifying/reflecting feelings. Permitting choice.	Relationship building. Improving self-esteem. Improving mood. Establishing a sense of control	Symbolic play. Permitting choice.	Correcting reality. Externalizing feelings. Taking initiative. Establishing own space.
GENERAL	PEGS. Identifying/reflecting feelings. Repetition compulsion	Re-establishing trust. Resolving emotional conflicts. Correcting reality	Repetition compulsion. Talking. Modeling. Behavioral rehearsal.	Externalizing and correcting specific conflict. Processing and problem solving. Skill development.

Games

Emphasis = Luck
Candy Land
Chutes 'n Ladders
Old Maid
Go Fish
Hungry Hippos

Emphasis = Luck + Skill
Trouble
Sorry
Conventional Card Games
Pac-Man

Emphasis = Skill
Checkers
Chess
Monopoly
Life
Battleship
Baseball
Darts
Football

Competition Vs. Cooperation

Aggression

Transference

Frustration Tolerance

Nurturance

Playroom Set-up

Equipment

- Child-size table with space for art materials, table top playhouse, dolls, and puppets

- Sandbox (floor), sand table or tray

- Some source of water

- Uncarpeted floor

- Carpeted floor and open space

- The elusive Bobo doll

Guidelines

- Room should be set up in the same way at the beginning of each session.

- Remove paintings, drawings, etc. left by previous clients.

- Children may not remove toys.

Basic Rules

- This is your special time. You may play with any of the toys in the room. You can play, talk, talk and play, or do nothing at all.

- You are not allowed to hurt yourself or me.

- You are not allowed to mess up yourself or me on purpose.

- You are not allowed to break toys on purpose or take them out of the room.

- Your time goes until ____ o'clock (or until the big hand is on the ____).

- You don't have to clean up unless you want to.

Axline's Eight Principles

1. Warm, friendly relationship.

2. Accept child as he/she is.

3. Establish a feeling of permissiveness.

4. Recognize and reflect feelings.

5. Respect child's ability to solve problems.

6. Do not direct child's actions.

7. Trust the process.

8. Establish limits which provide a reality anchor.

Nordling & Guerney (1999)

Warm-up

Aggressive

Regressive

Mastery

Playroom Setup

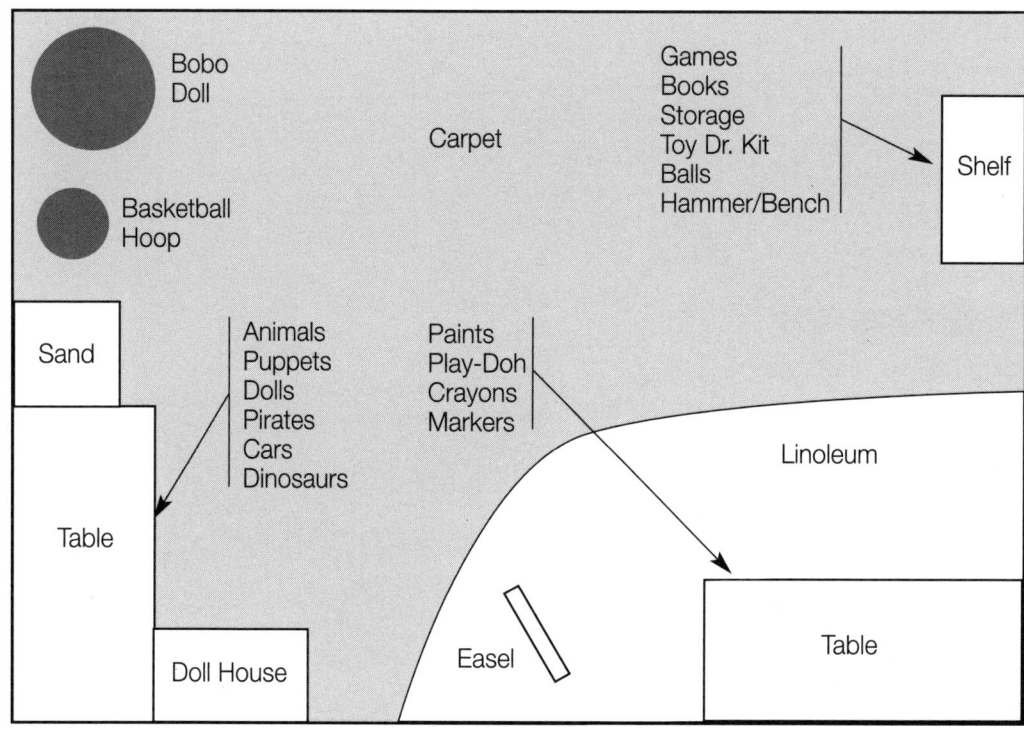

Chapter 13

Troubleshooting

This chapter is devoted to common questions I encounter in classes and workshops – the "what if's" that people think about when they are starting out. It is important to realize that most of these questions are related to anxiety, particularly if you haven't worked with children before. In addition, whenever someone is engaging in a new behavior, be it play therapy or dancing, it takes time to develop a sense of self-efficacy; that is, the belief that you can successfully perform the task. My assumption is that most people reading this book will be new to play therapy and, thus, low on self-efficacy in this area. When this is the case, individuals usually want to be prepared for as many potential problems as possible as a means of compensating for their still to be developed self-confidence. The purpose of this chapter is to provide this type of preparatory information.

Problems in Getting Started

What if I can't explain play therapy clearly to parents? Parent collaboration is a necessary element of counseling children. Thus, educating parents about what you will be doing with their children is important. If you don't think that you can do this adequately face-to-face, then provide the parents with something in writing, such as a pamphlet or summary on what you do in play therapy. An excellent resource for this is *The Child's First Book of Play Therapy* (Nemiroff & Annunziata, 1990), published by the American Psychological Association. If you work with parents who have poor reading skills, you might even use videotape resources, such as Nancy Boyd Webb's (1992), "Techniques of Play Therapy," or produce a simple video yourself with a pretend client.

What if the child does absolutely nothing when we start the first session? This is more a problem if you are using a non-directive type of play therapy. If the child is directing the session, she can always choose to not do anything, and you need to respect that choice. This is part of my rule, "Mean what you say." It is the counselor's job to describe what he is observing. So, if you notice the child is looking around, describe that behavior. ("Looks like you are checking things out."). If the child is sitting quietly, describe what you think the child is doing ("Looks like you are thinking about what to do.") Be patient. Most children begin playing within a few minutes.

If a child does not respond after a longer period of time, I usually position myself farther away from the child, to provide the child with more space. If the child continues to sit quietly, I sometimes begin doing something else (such as reading or doing paperwork), and check in with the child periodically to see if she wants to do anything. When I do this, I still respect the child's choice to do nothing. The reason I take these two actions is that I have found that longer periods of silence are linked with extreme anxiety about the counseling situation and extreme needs to control the situation. By giving the child space, I help reduce anxiety that might be generated by close interpersonal contact, and by appearing to distract myself I remove the child from being the center of attention. The important thing is to understand and respect the child's need to not do anything, and to respond to it with congruent therapist behavior.

I should also note that I have rarely run into children who would not play at all, probably only five children out of literally hundreds I have seen. In general, the children who have adamantly chosen to do nothing have been children at the extreme: severely sexually abused children, severely neglected children, and children with significant attachment problems. Outside of these rare situations, most children will begin playing relatively soon after a period of non-activity, or will respond to the techniques I described above.

General Responding

What if I give the wrong response? New play therapists often worry that they will fail to respond appropriately to children's play. My only advice is, "don't worry, be happy." There are no exact, correct responses. If you adhere to an open, reflective response format, you will at worse, do no harm. You will not always be accurate in your responding – I'm not always accurate in responding. However, if you present yourself as warm and accepting of clients, they will provide you with corrective feedback, and then you will understand what the child is doing. One of the absolute delights of working with children is that, for the most part, they haven't developed the defenses that adult clients present. Hence, children are usually very willing to let you know that you were off target, which will help you respond more accurately in the future. Don't worry, be happy.

What if the child tells me I sound funny? Agree with her because that's her perception. It sounds funny to her. Then continue attending with your responses.

What if the child orders me around and has me do things for him? If the child is asking you to do things he can do, such as open up Play-Doh cans, you will have to determine if this is part of a control theme in the play, or if the child is unwilling to take initiative. If it is part of an ongoing control theme, I follow orders. If it is a lack of initiative, I encourage the child to do it himself.

What if the client gets upset and starts crying? In most cases, the counselor should attend to the upset directly and soothe the client. Sit next to the client, reflect his feelings, put your hand on his shoulder or back, and help him calm himself. If the upset has to do with discomfort with the counselor – that is, with proximity – give the client some space and seat yourself farther away from the client in the room.

Limitsetting

What if the child won't listen to me? This is usually more a therapist issue than a client issue. Even defiant children will conform to limits if the therapist is firm and consistent. Beginning therapists, particularly younger trainees who have little experience with children, often worry about this because they are still transitioning to perceiving themselves as adults. What they fail to understand is that kids see them as adults: to children, an adult is an adult. All the counse-lor needs to do is assert himself as an adult. This means that the therapist needs to state the limit and consequences clearly, and follow through with consequences.

What if the child won't leave the room when time is up? State that time is up two times. If the child continues to play, or insists that she wants to stay, take the child by the hand, state that time is up and she can play with a particular toy next time, walk to the door, turn out the light, leave with the child, and close the door behind you.

What if the child tests one limit after another without stopping? If a session turns into nonstop limit testing, you might have to resort to the final choices described in Chapter 3. By the middle of a session, you will have a reasonable idea whether or not anything therapeutic is happening. If not, try using time out first, before ending a session.

What if the child appears to be intentionally mean? If a child is doing things to intentionally hurt or mess the therapist, but claims that his/her actions are accidental, the therapist needs to comment on this. The comments need to provide the child with an understanding of the therapist's perceptions. "You are telling me this is an accident, but it feels to me like you are doing this on purpose because this is the third time you have hurt me. If you hurt me again, I have to believe you mean to, and you will have to stop playing with that." In other words, you treat this like an intentional limit testing situation.

What if the child wants to sit on my lap and cuddle? This is one of those limitsetting situations that require that the counselor protect the integrity of the relationship. While a few years back, this would not have been a problem, allowing clients to sit on your lap can be misconstrued, and, therefore, is not a behavior that most counselors should condone, even with very young children. In this situation, you need to establish a physical boundary that is acceptable. For instance, the client may sit next to you on the floor, but may not rub or climb on you.

What if the child swears? Cursing is not necessarily unacceptable in the playroom. It is often a way in which children exert control, experiment with being "bad," and see if the counselor will be accepting of them. When kids swear, I usually label the act as a reflection of their feeling, rather than repeating the swear word. For instance, "You are so angry that you swore," or, "I think you want to see what will happen in here if you swear." There are some situations in which you might have to establish a no swearing rule. At one point in my career, my office was next to the main office of a school, with only thin walls separating the rooms. In that case, I had to limit swearing because of complaints from the secretaries. Also, if a counselor is so uncomfortable with swearing that it interferes with the counseling relationship, then he would have to be genuine, share this with the client, and establish a limit regarding swearing.

What if the client self-stimulates? Most counselors will, on occasion, work with children who inappropriately masturbate. Counselors who work primarily with sexually abused children will see this more often, while counselors who work with a more general population will see this infrequently. Self-stimulation of this kind is one of the symptoms of sexual abuse, but not always. It is a normal developmental phenomena for very young children to touch their genital areas from time to time (Drewes, 1999). This only becomes a problem when it occurs frequently and in inappropriate settings. It is unusual for older children to self-stimulate, which is usually observed as rubbing the genital area on the edge of a table or desk, or even on another person. When this type of behavior occurs, it needs to be addressed, not only with the child, but with other adults who have contact with the child.

If a child begins self-stimulating consistently so that it is obvious that the child is masturbating, I usually matter-of-factly ask the child to stop. I then share my feelings of discomfort with the client and explain that this is not the place to engage in that behavior. I also state that when people touch themselves in this way, they do it in a private place, not in public with other people around. I ask the child how he feels and why he thinks he touches himself (rubs on the table, etc.). After that, whenever the child exhibits any behavior that appears to be stimulating, I ask him to stop, using ACT language, "The playroom is not for touching yourself in."

As I stated above, this type of behavior is problematic and does require that the counselor investigate further. While sexual abuse is a concern, self-stimulation can also be a sign of genital infection, compulsive behavior, and poor social skills, to name just a few possibilities. In schools, it is a good idea to consult with the school nurse and speak with parents regarding your concerns. If you have some doubts about what you are observing, seek advice from a counseling colleague. In agency or private settings, informing parents and requesting a medical consultation is the prudent course of action. While I don't automatically assume that a child has been sexually abused, I prefer to be conservative and request a second opinion regarding the reason for the behavior.

OTHER ISSUES

What if a teacher directs me to discuss a specific problem with a child, even if this is not part of the therapy? In this case, you need to be more strategic in order to avoid disrespecting both the teacher and the child. What I usually do is tell the child that the *teacher* has asked me to bring this up and that the child may *choose* to talk about this or *choose not* to. Then, I redirect the session to the play therapy. At the end of the session, I can then tell the teacher that we discussed the issue, but cannot disclose the discussion because of confidentiality.

What if the client accidentally hurts herself? When clients accidentally hurt themselves to the extent that they are upset, it is the counselor's responsibility to soothe them. This is part of the role of being the Good Mother. So, take care of the "booboo," rub the client's back, take her to the nurse if necessary, and help calm her.

What if the child does not want to terminate therapy, even though the child has resolved the therapeutic issues? This is where the counselor needs to keep focused on the endpoint and reinforce the child's gains. At the same time the counselor needs to attend to the child's feelings regarding termination, and to help the child understand that her desire to continue is related to her feelings of loss. The counselor also needs to reassure the child that there are other ways that the child can stay in contact with the counselor (cards, pictures, letters, etc.).

REFERENCES

Allen, J., & Berry, P. (1987). Sandplay. *Elementary School Guidance & Counseling, 21,* 300-306.

Appel, K. (1931). Drawings of children as aids in personality studies. *American Journal of Orthopsychiatry, 1,* 129-144.

Arlow, J. (1989). Psychoanalysis. In R. Corsini (Ed.), *Current Psychotherapies,* 4th Ed. Itasca, IL: F.E. Peacock.

Axline, V. (1947). *Play therapy: The inner dynamics of childhood.* Boston: Houghton Mifflin.

Axline, V. (1964). *Dibs in search of self.* New York: Ballantine Books.

Bandura, A. (1973). *Aggression: A social learning analysis.* Englewood Cliffs, NJ: Prentice-Hall.

Barlow, K., Strother, J., & Landreth, G. (1985). Child-centered play therapy: Nancy from baldness to curls. *The School Counselor, 32,* 347-356.

Berger, K. (1991). *The developing person through childhood and adolescence.* New York: Worth.

Bettelheim, B. (1987). The importance of play. *The Atlantic Monthly* (March), 35-46.

Bleck, R., & Bleck, B. (1982). The disruptive child's play group. *Elementary School Guidance & Counseling, 17,* 137-141.

Bonner, B., & Everett, F. (1986). Influence of client preparation and problem severity on attitudes and expectations in child psychotherapy. *Professional Psychology: Research and Practice, 17,* 223-229.

Brody, V. (1997). Developmental play therapy. In K. O'Connor & L. Braverman (Eds.), *Play therapy theory and practice: A comparative presentation (pp.160-183).* New York: Wiley.

Brooks, R. (1981). Creative characters: A technique in child therapy. *Psychotherapy: Theory, Research and Practice, 18* (1), 131-139.

Burns, R., & Kaufman, S. (1970). *Kinetic family drawings (K-F-D): An introduction to understanding children through kinetic drawing.* New York: Brunner/Mazel.

Carkhuff, R., & Berenson, B. (1977). *Beyond counseling and therapy,* 2nd. Ed. New York: Holt, Rinehart and Winston.

Carmichael, K. (1991). Play therapy: Role in reading improvement. *Reading Improvement, 28,* 273-276.

Carter, S. (1987). Use of puppets to treat traumatic grief: A case study. *Elementary School Guidance & Counseling, 21,* 210-215.

Cerio, J. (1989). Pre-counseling orientation of elementary school children. *Dissertation Abstracts International, 49.*

Cerio, J. (1993). A comparison of cognitive and affective methods of precounseling orientation. *New York State Journal for Counseling & Development, 8,* 55-63.

Cerio, J. (1999). Future directions in play therapy research. *Journal for the Professional Counselor, 14,* 80-86.

Cerio, J., Taggart, T., & Costa, L. (1999). Play therapy training practices for school counselors: Results of a national study. *Journal for the Professional Counselor, 14,* 55-65.

Chau, I., & Landreth, G. (1997). Filial therapy with Chinese parents: Effects on parental empathic interactions, parental acceptance of child and parental stress. *International Journal of Play Therapy, 6,* 75-92.

Crow, J. (1994). *Play therapy with low achievers in reading.* University of Louisville. (ERIC# ED375358).

Day, L, & Reznikoff, M. (1980). Preparation of children and parents for treatment at a children's psychiatric clinic through videotaped modeling. *Journal of Consulting and Clinical Psychology, 48,* 303-304.

Dewey, J. (1938). *Experience and Education.* New York: MacMillan.

Dinkmeyer, D. (1973). *Developing understanding of self and others:* D-2. Circle Pines, MN: American Guidance Service.

Donovan, D., & McIntyre, D. (1990). *Healing the hurt child.* New York: W.W. Norton.

Doster, J. (1975). Individual differences affecting interviewee expectancies and perceptions of self-disclosure. *Journal of Counseling Psychology, 22,* 192-198.

Drewes, A. (1999). Developmental considerations in play and play therapy with traumatized children. *Journal of the Professional Counselor, 14,* 35-52.

Egan, G. (1994). *The skilled helper: A problem management approach to helping,* 5th Ed. Pacific Grove, CA: Brooks/Cole.

Erikson, E. (1963). *Childhood and society,* 2nd. Ed. New York: W.W. Norton.

Francois, T. (1977). *The engagement of adolescent black males in psychotherapy: The relation of role induction, locus of control, and depression.* Unpublished dissertation, New York University.

Frank, J., Gliedman, L., Imber, S., Stone, A., & Nash, E. (1959). Patient's expectancies and relearning as factors determining improvement in psychotherapy. *American Journal of Psychiatry, 115,* 961-968.

Gardner, R. (1971). *Therapeutic communication with children: The mutual storytelling technique.* Northvale, NJ: Jason Aronson.

Gay, L. (1976). *Educational research: Competencies for analysis and application.* Columbus, OH: Charles C. Merrill.

Gazda, G., Childers, W., & Brooks, D. (1987). *Foundations of counseling and human services.* New York: McGraw-Hill.

Gil, E. (1991). *The healing power of play: Working with abused children.* New York: Guilford.

Gilmore, J. (1971). The effectiveness of parental counseling with other modalities in the treatment of children with learning disabilities. *Journal of Education, 154,* 74-82.

Glass, N. (1987). Parents as therapeutic agents: A study of the effect of filial therapy. *Dissertation Abstracts International, 47* (07): A2457.

Griffiths, A. (1971). Self-concept in remedial work with dyslexic children. *Academic Therapy, 2,* 125-133.

Gunnison, H. (1975). Creed of a counselor. *Personnel and Guidance Journal, 54,* 143.

Gunnison, H. (1990). Hypnocounseling: Ericksonian hypnosis for counselors. *Journal of Counseling and Development, 68,* 450-453.

Gunnison, H. (1999). *Hypnocounseling: An eclectic bridge.* Unpublished manuscript.

Haley, J. (1976). *Problem-solving therapy.* New York: Harper-Colophon Books.

Henderson, P. (1987). Terminating the counseling relationship with children. *Elementary School Guidance & Counseling, 22,* 143-148.

Hendricks, S. (1971). *A descriptive analysis of the process of client-centered play therapy.* (DAI 32/07A). Unpublished doctoral dissertation: University of North Texas.

Herring, R. (1997). *Counseling diverse ethnic youth.* New York: Harcourt Brace College Publishers.

Holloway, E. (1995). *Clinical supervision: A systems approach.* Thousand Oaks, CA: Sage.

Holmes, D., & Urie, R. (1975). Effects of preparing children for psychotherapy. *Journal of Consulting and Clinical Psychology, 43,* 311-318.

Hoyt, R. (1979). *Effects of pretherapy role induction interviews upon treatment expectations and outcome in brief psychotherapy.* Unpublished dissertation. Ohio University.

Ivey, A., & Ivey, M. (1999). *Intentional interviewing & counseling: Facilitating client development in a multicultural society,* 4th Ed. Pacific Grove, CA: Brooks/Cole.

James, R., & Myer, R. (1987). Puppets: The elementary school counselor's right or left arm. *Elementary School Guidance & Counseling, 21,* 292-299.

Jernberg, A. (1979). *Theraplay*. San Francisco: Jossey-Bass.

Kamphaus, R., & Frick, P. (1996). *Clinical assessment of child and adolescent personality and behavior*. Boston: Allyn and Bacon.

Kaplewicz, N.L. (1999). *Effects of group play therapy on reading achievement and emotional symptoms among remedial readers*. Unpublished dissertation. Alfred University.

Koppitz, E. (1968). *Psychological evaluation of children's human figure drawings*. New York: Grune & Stratton.

Korchin, S. (1980). Clinical psychology and minority problems. *American Psychologist, 35*, 262-269.

Lambert, M., & Bergin, A. (1994). The effectiveness of psychotherapy. In A. Bergin & S. Garfield (Eds.), *Handbook of Psychotherapy and Behavior Change*, 4th Ed. (143-189) New York: John C. Wiley & Sons.

Landreth, G. (1987). Play therapy: Facilitative use of child's play in elementary school counseling. *Elementary School Guidance & Counseling, 22*, 253-261.

Landreth, G. (1991). *Play therapy: The art of the relationship*. Muncie, IN: Accelerated Development.

Lazare, A., Eisenthal, S., & Wasserman, L. (1975). The customer approach to patienthood: Attending to patient requests in a walk-in clinic. *Archives of General Psychiatry, 32*, 553-559.

Lee, C. (1995). *Counseling for diversity*. Boston: Allyn & Bacon.

Levy, S. (1984). *Principles of interpretation*. New York: Aronson.

McGoldrick, M., & Gerson, R. (1985). *Genograms in family assessment*. New York: Norton.

Mehrabian, A. (1971). *Silent messages*. Belmont, CA: Wadsworth.

Meichenbaum, D. (1977). *Cognitive-behavior modification: An integrative approach*. New York: Plenum Press.

Mills, J., & Crowley, R. (1986). *Therapeutic metaphors for children and the child within*. New York: Brunner/Mazel.

Minuchin, S., & Fishman, C. (1981). *Family therapy techniques*. Cambridge, MA: Harvard University Press.

Moustakas, C. (1959). *Psychotherapy with children: The living relationship*. New York: Ballantine Books.

Naglieri, J., McNeish, T., & Bardos, A. (1991). *Draw-a-person: Screening procedure for emotional disturbance*. Austin, TX: PRO-ED.

Nemiroff, M., & Annunziata, J. (1990). *A child's first book about play therapy*. Washington, DC: American Psychological Association.

Nickerson, E., & O'Laughlin, K. (1983). The therapeutic use of games. In C. Schaefer & K. O'Connor (Eds.), *Handbook of Play Therapy* (pp. 174-187). New York: John C. Wiley & Son.

Nordling, W., & Guerney, L. (1999). Typical stages in the Child-centered play therapy process. *Journal for the Professional Counselor, 14*, 16-22.

Oaklander, V. (1992). Gestalt work with children: Working with anger. In E.C. Nevins, Ed., *Gestalt Therapy: Perspectives and Applications*. New York: Gardner Press.

O'Connor, K. (1991). *The play therapy primer*. New York: John Wiley & Son.

O'Connor, K., & Braverman, L. (Eds.) (1997). *Play therapy theory and practice: A comparative presentation*. New York: John C. Wiley & Sons.

Oster, G., & Gould, P. (1987). *Using drawings in assessment and therapy*. New York: Brunner/Mazel.

Park, W., & Williams, G. (1986). Encouraging elementary school children to refer themselves for counseling. *Elementary School Guidance and Counseling, 21*, 8-14.

Pedersen, P. (1984). The cultural complexity of mental health. In P. Pedersen, N. Sartorius, & A. Marsella (Eds.), *Mental health services* (pp. 13-27). Beverly Hills, CA: Sage.

Pedersen, P. (1988). *A handbook for developing multicultural awareness.* Alexandria, VA: American Association for Counseling and Development.

Pedersen, P. (1991). Multiculturalism as a generic approach to counseling. *Journal of Counseling & Development, 70,* 6-12.

Piaget, J. (1962). *Play, dreams and imitation in childhood.* New York: W.W. Norton.

Reid, W. (1980). *Basic intensive psychotherapy.* New York: Brunner/Mazel.

Reynolds, C., & Kamphaus, R. (1992). *Behavior assessment system for children.* Circle Pines, MN: American Guidance Service.

Rogers, C. (1957). The necessary and sufficient conditions for therapeutic personality change. *Journal of Consulting Psychology, 25,* 95-103.

Rogers, C. (1961). *On becoming a person.* Boston: Houghton-Mifflin.

Rogers, C. (1965). Client-centered therapy. Part I. In E. Shostrom (Ed.), *Three approaches to psychotherapy.* [Film]. Santa Ana CA: Psychological Films.

Rogers, C. (1975). Empathic: An unappreciated way of being. *The Counseling Psychologist, 5,* 2-10.

Schaefer, C., & O'Connor, K. (Eds.) (1983). *Handbook of play therapy.* New York: John Wiley & Son.

Schaefer, C., & Reid, S. (Eds.) (1986). *Game play: Therapeutic use of childhood games.* New York: John C. Wiley & Sons.

Sledge, W. (1977). The therapist's use of metaphor. *International Journal of Psychoanalytic Psychotherapy, 6,* 113-130.

Sloan, S. (1997). *Effects of therapeutic aggressive play: Does it increase or diminish spontaneous aggression?* Unpublished doctoral dissertation. Alfred University.

Strupp, H., & Bloxom, A. (1973). Preparing lower-class patients for group psychotherapy: Development and evaluation of a role-induction film. *Journal of Consulting and Clinical Psychology, 41,* 373-384.

Sue, D.W., & Sue, D. (1977). Barriers to effective cross-cultural counseling. *Journal of Counseling Psychology, 24,* 420-429.

Sue, D.W., & Sue, D. (1990). *Counseling the culturally different: Theory and practice.* New York: Wiley.

Sue, S. (1977). Community mental health services to minority groups: Some optimism, some pessimism. *American Psychologist, 32,* 616-624.

Swartz, S., & Swartz, J. (1985). *Counseling the disabled reader.* Paper presented at the Annual Meeting of the Illinois Council for Exceptional Children. ERIC# ED265689.

Sydnor, G., Akridge, R., & Parkhill, N. (1972). *Human relations training: A programmed manual.* Minden, LA: Human Resources Development Training Institute.

Taggart, T., & Cerio, J. (1999). *Play therapy: Do school psychologists practice what trainers teach?* Unpublished manuscript.

Trostle, S. (1988). The effects of child-centered group play sessions on the social-emotional growth of three to six year old bilingual Puerto Rican children. *Journal of Research in Childhood Education, 3,* 93-106.

Truax, C., & Carkhuff, R. (1967). *Toward effective counseling and psychotherapy.* Chicago: Aldine.

Vinturella, L., & James, R. (1987). Sand play: A therapeutic medium with children. *Elementary School Guidance & Counseling, 21,* 229-238.

Watkins, C.E. (1985). Countertransference: Its impact on the counseling situation. *Journal of Counseling and Development, 63,* 356-359.

Webb, N.B. (1992). *Techniques of play therapy.* [Film]. New York: Guilford.

Williams, K. (1996). *Relationships among DAP:SPED indicators, self-report anxiety and depression scores and behavior ratings of children ages 8-11*. Unpublished dissertation, Alfred University.

Whitaker, C., & Bumberry, W. (1988). *Dancing with the family: A symbolic-experiential approach*. New York: Brunner/Mazel.

Wolff, W. (1942). Projective methods for personality analysis of expressive behavior in pre-school children. *Character & Personality, 10*, 309-330.

Yalom, I. (1985). *The theory and practice of group psychotherapy*. New York: Basic Books.

Zarchan, D. (1977). *Effects of social class and role-induction on dropout expectations and attraction in out-patient psychotherapy*. Unpublished dissertation, Boston University.

Zins, J., Maher, C., Murphy, J., & Wess, B. (1988). The peer support group: A means to facilitate professional development. *School Psychology Review, 17*, 138-146.

Zwick, R., & Attkisson, C. (1985). Effectiveness of a client pretherapy orientation videotape. *Journal of Counseling Psychology, 32*, 514-524.

Author Index

Akridge, R., 13
Allen, J., 116
Annunziata, J., 151
Appel, K., 53
Arlow, J., 75, 89
Attkisson, C., 50
Axline, V., vii, 2, 72, 127, 133, 143, 148
Bandura, A., 5
Bardos, A., 53
Barlow, K., 125
Berenson, B., 11, 13, 14, 81, 82, 85
Berger, K., 41
Bergin, A., 12, 105
Berry, P., 116
Bettelheim, B., 1, 5
Bleck, B., 127
Bleck, R., 127
Bloxom, A., 50
Bonner, B., 50
Braverman, L., 11
Brody, V., 90
Brooks, D., 100
Brooks, R., 116
Bumberry, W., viii, 115, 120, 128
Burns, R., 53
Carkhuff, R., 11, 13, 14, 81, 82, 85
Carmichael, K., 127
Carter, S., 117
Cerio, J., 50, 53, 58, 100, 125, 139
Chau, I., 46
Childers, W., 100
Costa, L., 100, 139
Crowley, R., 116
Day, L., 50, 134
Dewey, J., 136
Dinkmeyer, D., 117
Donovan, D., vii
Doster, J., 50
Drewes, A., 153
Egan, G., 11, 81, 95
Eisenthal, S., 40
Erikson, E., 1, 2, 4, 65, 85, 143
Everett, F., 50
Fishman, C., 126
Francois, T., 50
Frank, J., 50
Frick, P., 53
Gardner, R., 115, 116
Gay, L., 41, 125
Gazda, G., 100
Gerson, R., 53
Gil, E., vii
Gilmore, J., 127
Glass, N., 127
Gliedman, L., 50
Gould, P., 52
Griffiths, A., 127
Guerney, L., 83, 143
Gunnison, H., 12, 45, 71, 115, 120
Haley, J., 115, 120
Henderson, P., 125
Hendricks, S., 86
Herring, R., 40
Holloway, E., 101, 102
Holmes, D., 50, 134
Hoyt, R., 50, 134
Imber, S., 50
Ivey, A., 11
Ivey, M., 11
James, R., 116, 117

Jernberg, A., 84, 85, 128, 129
Kaufman, S., 53
Kamphaus, R., 53, 125
Kaplewicz, N. L., 105
Koppitz, E., 53
Korchin, S., 40
Lambert, M., 12, 105
Landreth, G., vii, viii,1, 3, 5,11, 15, 25, 26, 28, 46, 49, 60, 105, 125
Lazare, A., 40
Lee, C., 40
Levy, S., 75
Maher, C., 101
McGoldrick, M., 53
McIntyre, D., vii
McNeish, T., 53
Mehrabian, A., 11
Meichenbaum, D., 112
Mills, J., 116
Minuchin, S., 126
Moustakas, C., vii,143
Murphy, J., 101
Myer, R., 117
Naglieri, J., 53
Nash, E., 50
Nemiroff, M., 151
Nickerson, E., 66
Nordling, W., 83, 149
Oaklander, V., 5
O'Connor, K., vii, viii, 1, 11, 90, 98, 125, 128
O'Laughlin, K., 66
Oster, G., 52
Park, W., 50, 58
Parkhill, N., 13
Pedersen, P., 40

Piaget, J., 2
Reid, S., 5, 60
Reid, W., 100
Reynolds, C., 125
Reznikoff, M., 50, 134
Rogers, C., 1, 11, 12, 72, 73, 89, 98
Schaefer, C., vii, viii, 5, 60
Sledge, W., 116
Sloan, S., 86
Stone, A., 50
Strother, J., 125
Strupp, H., 50
Sue, D., 40, 46
Sue, D.W., 40,46
Sue, S., 40
Swartz, J., 127
Swartz, S., 127
Sydnor, G., 13, 14
Taggart, T., 100, 139
Trostle, S., 46
Truax, C., 11, 13
Urie, R., 50, 134
Vinturella, L., 116
Wasserman, L., 40
Watkins, C.E., 95
Webb, N.B., 151
Wess, B., 101
Whitaker, C., viii, 115, 120, 128, 133
Williams, G., 50, 58
Williams, K., 53
Wolff, W., 53
Yalom, I., 127
Zarchan, D., 50
Zins, J., 101
Zwick, R., 50

ABOUT THE AUTHOR

Jay Cerio is a professor of School Psychology at Alfred University in western New York State, and director of the university's Child and Family Services Center, a full service child guidance clinic. A licensed psychologist, certified school psychologist, and certified school counselor, Jay has been a practitioner of play therapy for 25 years in school and clinical settings. He has authored numerous articles on play therapy, family therapy, and counselor training, and has an ongoing research program on play therapy in progress at Alfred University. Jay is a regular workshop presenter at national and regional conferences and an active consultant with schools and mental health agencies.